IMAGES
of America

SOUTH
PLAINFIELD

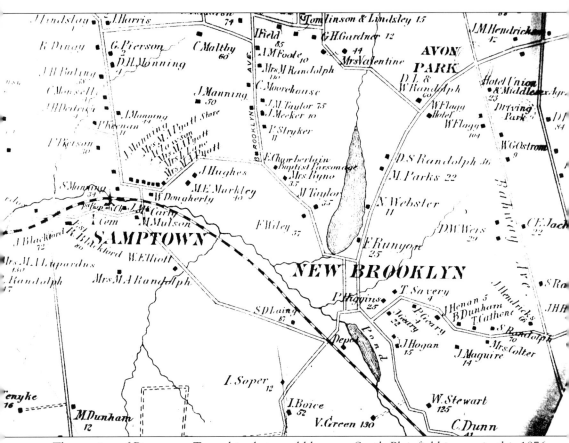

The portion of Piscataway Township that would become South Plainfield is seen in this 1876 map, first published in the Everts and Stewart *Combination Atlas Map of Middlesex County, New Jersey*. Samptown and New Brooklyn are shown, as well as Spring Lake, the sawmill pond, and many individual farms.

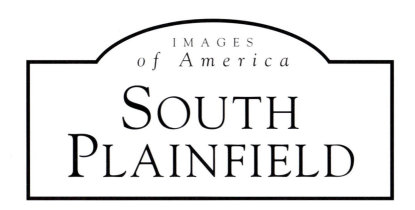

IMAGES of America
SOUTH PLAINFIELD

Richard F. Veit

Copyright © 2002 by Richard F. Veit.
ISBN 0-7385-1111-0

First printed in 2002.

Published by Arcadia Publishing,
an imprint of Tempus Publishing, Inc.
2A Cumberland Street
Charleston, SC 29401

Printed in Great Britain.

Library of Congress Catalog Card Number: 2002109302

For all general information contact Arcadia Publishing at:
Telephone 843-853-2070
Fax 843-853-0044
E-Mail sales@arcadiapublishing.com

For customer service and orders:
Toll-Free 1-888-313-2665

Visit us on the internet at http://www.arcadiapublishing.com

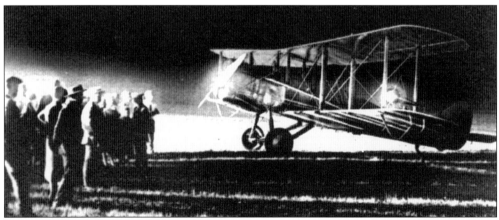

This ethereal photograph shows an early airmail flight from Hadley Field on August 2, 1925. Notice the large landing lights on the wingtips of the U.S. Air Mail Service airplane. At this point, Hadley Field was quite literally a field. (Reproduced courtesy of the Air Mail Pioneers.)

CONTENTS

Acknowledgments		6
Introduction		7
1.	Samptown and New Brooklyn: Crossroads Towns	9
2.	Rural Life in Central Jersey	37
3.	Transformed by the Railroad	53
4.	Industry Builds South Plainfield	61
5.	Hadley Airfield	71
6.	In Service	83
7.	School Days	101
8.	Suburbanization	113

Acknowledgments

This book would not have been written without the assistance of several key people. My parents, Maryann and Richard F. Veit Sr., encouraged my interest in history, and particularly local history, from an early age. Terri, my wife, put up with hours of absence as I gathered information and photographs and compiled this book. Dorothy and Sarah Miele, an amazing mother-daughter team, beat the bushes for old photographs of South Plainfield. Without their help, the photographic record presented here would not be half as rich. Larry Randolph, longtime champion of South Plainfield's history, shared useful sources, photographs, and his critical insights into the history of the borough. The South Plainfield Historical Society allowed me to work with and share its extensive collection of historic materials, while the South Plainfield Public Library shared its historic aerial photographs. The South Plainfield Fire Department provided generous access to its rich photographic archive. I particularly appreciated the help of Douglas Tackach Jr. My brother, Greg Veit, helped identify many of the early airplanes in the Hadley Field photographs. Tim McConville, my brother-in-law, helped reproduce some of the photographs. Local resident, Robert Bengivenga, shared his family's rich photograph collection. Margorie Reedy, a descendant of the Dunham and Norman families, welcomed me into her home and allowed me to copy some of the earliest extant photographs of South Plainfield. William Ball found a set of early aerial photos that show the rural South Plainfield of a century ago. Retired police officer Jake Cataldo and current officer Kevin Murtagh provided early photographs of the South Plainfield Police Department. Maria Vajo, of the Metuchen-Edison Historical Society, guided me to the South Plainfield photographs in the J. Lloyd Grimstead collection. Bruce Hadley shared some outstanding photographs of the Hadley farm, which later became Hadley Field. Arcadia author, Bruce Ryno, of North Plainfield, lent some excellent photographs of historic houses and schools, as well as pertinent historical information. Director Joseph DaRold and Jessica Myers, both of the Plainfield Public Library, provided gracious access to the magnificent Collier collection. Jean Kolva, of the Highland Park Historical Society, shared an interesting collection of tax photographs from the 1940s. Frances Romeo lent some early snapshots of historic houses. The Dana Corporation, Harris Steel, and the Harness Racing Museum and Hall of Fame provided photographs from their collections. Randy Gabriellan, Arcadia author extraordinaire, shared his insights into the process of writing a town history. The Special Collections and Archives at Rutgers University was, as usual, the source for information on all things New Jersey. Thanks are also due to Dean William Mitchell and Dr. Brian Greenberg of Monmouth University, two colleagues who have encouraged my interest in local history. My editor at Arcadia Publishing, Susie Jaggard, was a pleasure to work with. To everyone else who shared photographs, postcards, and insights into the history of the town, thank you.

INTRODUCTION

South Plainfield is located in northwestern Middlesex County. In 2000, the town had a population of 21,810. The borough has a surface area of 8.2 square miles. Its landscape takes the form of a shallow basin. To the east, a low ridge of hills running along Woodland Avenue form part of the terminal moraine where the Wisconsin glacier stopped its advance roughly 15,000 years ago. The Bound Brook and its tributaries run through South Plainfield. Wetlands bordering these watercourses were valuable to Native American hunters and gatherers. Archaeological sites dating back 8,000 years have been found along the wetlands. South Plainfield's first inhabitants were Native Americans, predecessors of the later Lenape.

In 1664, today's South Plainfield was included as part of the Elizabethtown Purchase. Settlement of the area, then part of Piscataway, began in 1666. Some early settlers, such as eastern New Jersey proprietor John Barclay, were Quakers of Scottish descent who suffered persecution in the Old World. Others were second-generation immigrants who hailed from New England. Another early settler was John Laing, a Quaker whose house still stands just across the township line in Edison. Local Quakers built a meetinghouse in the 1730s, which is believed to have stood in South Plainfield in the area between Maple Avenue and the Police Athletic League Building. The cemetery associated with the meetinghouse remained until the early 20th century. Laing's plantation was apparently called Plainfield, though there is debate as to whether this refers to the plain dress of the Quakers or the local landscape. Whichever was the case, it was the inspiration for the names of Plainfield, South Plainfield, and North Plainfield. In 1788, the Quakers relocated their meetinghouse to Plainfield, where it remains today.

Other pre-Revolutionary settlers included the Blackford, Drake, Dunn, Dunham, Hull, Manning, Martin, Randolph, Runyon, Stelle, and Ten Eyck families. Many were Baptists from Massachusetts and Maine; others were French Huguenots. In the 1680s, a sawmill was established in town, and shortly thereafter the Bound Brook was dammed to form Spring Lake, which powered a gristmill. The name Samptown, first used in the 17th century, derives from a Native American word for ground cornmeal. Another early name for the area was Waterville.

During the Revolutionary War, extensive skirmishing took place in and around South Plainfield as the British army gathered forage and attempted to lure Washington into a full-scale battle. Hessian, British, and American diaries note fighting in Quibbletown, today's New Market, and Samptown. After the war, the future South Plainfield returned to a largely agrarian existence. In 1792, the Samptown Baptist Church was established, splitting off from the Scotch Plains Baptist Church. The church was located in the Waterville, or Samptown, Cemetery. Its first pastor was the Reverend Jacob Fitz-Randolph.

Over the course of the 19th century, the importance of Samptown declined as that of Brooklyn or New Brooklyn grew. New Brooklyn was closer to the mills and had a store and schoolhouse. When a spark from a passing steam engine set the old Baptist church on fire in 1879, a replacement was constructed in New Brooklyn. This building still stands. The Lehigh Valley Railroad laid its tracks through the town in 1875 and constructed a massive coal yard on the south side of town. The railroad opened up South Plainfield to the outside world, and industries soon began to locate along the tracks. One of the first to move here was the Spicer Manufacturing Company, which purchased the Elliot farm in 1913. Spicer built a substantial plant to manufacture universal joints, axles, and other components of early cars. Shortly thereafter, Harris Structural Steel purchased the Blackford farm and erected a massive steel fabrication plant. Later, in 1936, Cornell Dubilier, an electronics manufacturer, purchased the Spicer plant.

The name South Plainfield was used as early as the 1870s, and a South Plainfield post office was established in 1887. The switch from New Brooklyn to South Plainfield probably relates to the growing importance of Plainfield, the leading regional commercial center of the time. At the turn of the century, entrepreneur Milton Mendell developed a small resort on what had been Colonel Holly's estate. He called it Holly Park. South Plainfield also had two horse tracks in the early 20th century; one off Tompkins Avenue and another near Park Avenue. By this time, the community had developed a rather mixed reputation. Despite a growing population, it lacked any sort of organized police force, fire department, or government. Taverns served customers seven days a week and drew crowds from neighboring communities, which had blue laws. On May 17, 1907, the Middlesex Volunteer Fire Company, subsequently renamed the South Plainfield Volunteer Fire Company, was organized. Despite firefighters' valiant efforts, two years later, on January 6, 1909, the gristmill, a notable local landmark, burned down.

South Plainfield had its brush with fame in the 1920s, when the U.S. Post Office used Hadley Field, an airfield on John Hadley's farm, as the eastern terminus for its airmail flights. On July 1, 1925, the first transcontinental night airmail flight took off from Hadley Field. The airport closed in 1968.

The population continued to grow during the early 20th century as new waves of Irish, Italian, and eastern-European immigrants came to town drawn by the burgeoning industries. A Russian nobleman even attempted, with limited success, to establish a community for refugees from the Russian Revolution near Metuchen Road. New houses of worship, such as Sacred Heart Church and Our Lady of Czestochowa, served the needs of the growing population.

The Borough of South Plainfield officially separated from Piscataway Township on March 12, 1926. William Hamilton served as the first mayor. The community's growth slowed during the Depression and then exploded in the years immediately following World War II. Starting with the Geary Park subdivision, farm fields were transformed into suburbs. New schools were built to accommodate the growing number of students. The construction of Route 287 led to further growth.

Today, South Plainfield continues to grow and change. A new wave of immigrants, from Asia and Latin America, is adding to the community's diversity. Located at the crossroads of central New Jersey, South Plainfield's future will undoubtedly continue to be as rich and intriguing as its past.

One
SAMPTOWN AND NEW BROOKLYN: CROSSROADS TOWNS

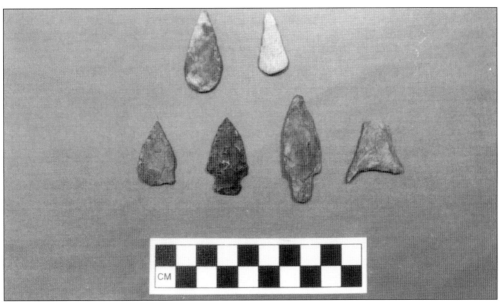

South Plainfield has a rich Native American heritage. These projectile points, arrowheads, and spearpoints were found at various locations in the borough. Those in the top row are characterized as teardrop points and date from the late Archaic period, roughly 5,000 years ago. The points in the bottom row are, from left to right, unidentified, a Brewerton side-notched point (3000–2000 B.C.), a Lamoka point (3500–2500 B.C.), and a Levanna point (A.D. 700–1350).

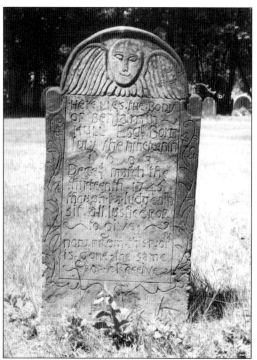

This photograph shows the gravestone of Judge Benjamin Hull (1693–1745). The gravestone is the oldest surviving marker in the Samptown Cemetery. Carved from red sandstone and decorated with a cherub, its epitaph reads, "Though I a judge did sit, all justice for to give, now from this world is gone, the same for to receive." Hull was a descendant of Hopewell Hull, one of the founders of Piscataway.

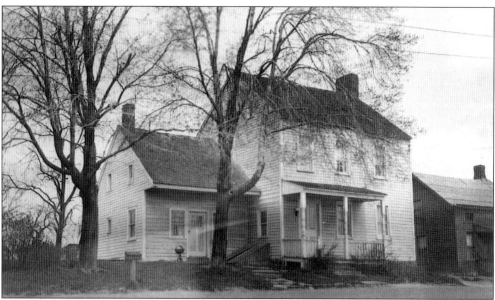

The Drake or Wesley-Drake House stands on Sampton Avenue and is believed to date from c. 1762. The house once stood at the center of Samptown. The section of the house on the left appears to be a Dutch cottage and is the oldest portion of the building. To the right is the side-hall-plan main block. At points in its history, it has served as a tavern, a stagecoach stop, and a store. Samuel Pyatt purchased the house in 1859. In 1919, Chester Wojciechowski, whose name was anglicized to Wesley, moved in. Samptown was a hamlet that was established in the early 18th century at a crossing over the Bound Brook. (Reproduced courtesy of the Metuchen-Edison Historical Society.)

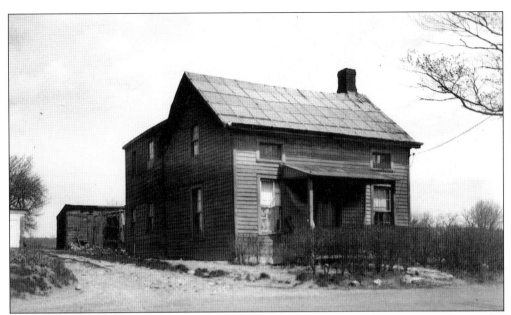

This weather-beaten house with a tin roof stood just east of the Drake House. Part of Samptown, this house likely dates from the 19th century. Notice the shed or outhouse behind the house, and the painted outhouse from the Drake House is seen on the left. S. Manning owned the house when J. Lloyd Grimstead photographed it in the early 20th century. At one point, it was a wing of the Drake House and also served as a grocery store. (Reproduced courtesy of the Metuchen-Edison Historical Society.)

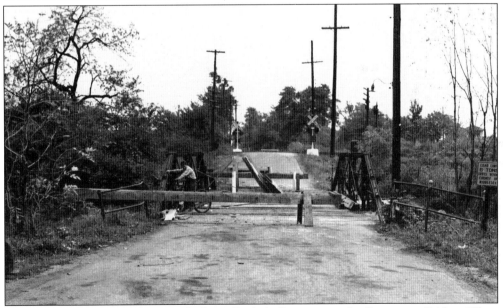

This early-20th-century photograph shows Drake's Crossing, or the Samptown Bridge. When this photograph was taken, the small trestle bridge was apparently blocked to automobile traffic but remained open to pedestrians and bicyclists. Today, a concrete bridge spans the Bound Brook, or as it is more commonly known, New Market Creek. The view is looking south along the Clinton Avenue extension.

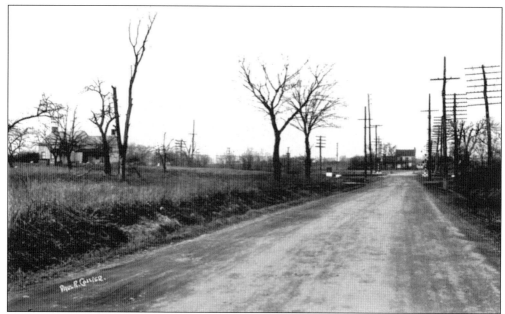

This photograph, taken in the late fall or winter, shows the Drake House in the distance. To the left is the Mullinson, or Mulson, house, another 18th-century structure. Hessian and American troops skirmished here during the Revolution. Paul Collier, a prominent Plainfield photographer, took the photograph in the 1920s. (Reproduced courtesy of the Plainfield Public Library, Paul Revere Collier Collection, donation of William T. Garrett.)

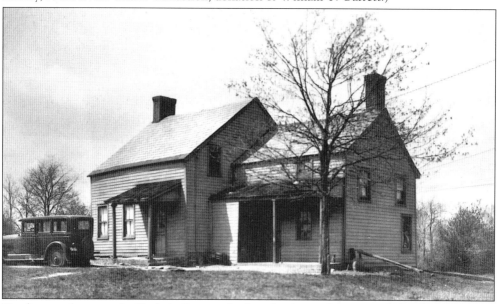

Heading south across the Drake's Crossing bridge, this house, known as the Mullinson house, would have stood on the right. Today, the low hill it stood on has been graded away and replaced by a gravel parking lot. This is a Grimstead photograph from the 1930s. Grimstead, a Metuchen photographer who was active in the early 20th century, created an amazingly detailed photographic record of the Central Jersey he knew. (Reproduced courtesy of the Metuchen-Edison Historical Society.)

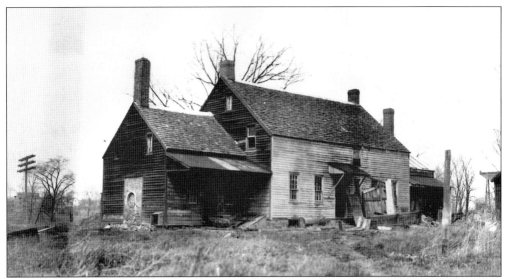

The cranes of Harris Steel, visible at the far right in this photograph, give a hint about the location. The J. Blackford house was one of two houses associated with the Blackford family that stood into the 20th century. The house dated from the 18th century. Notice the collapsed brick-baking oven on the kitchen wing to the left. The photograph dates from 1936. (Reproduced courtesy of the Metuchen-Edison Historical Society.)

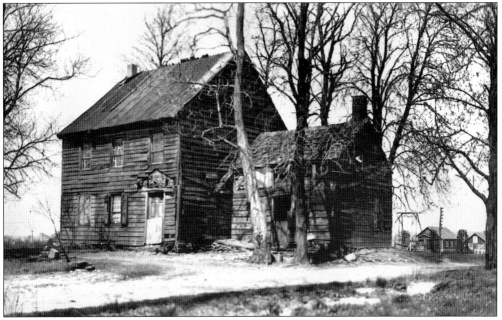

This photograph shows the C. Blackford house. The Blackfords were an important early family who first settled in Piscataway in 1685. This house also stood near Harris Steel. Company housing built for Harris Steel employees is visible to the right of the house. The main block of the house is a side-hall-plan structure. This form was popular in the late 18th and early 19th centuries. Charles Anthony purchased the farmhouse in 1936, and it stood until 1939. Anthony had hoped to restore the house but was unable to secure the necessary loans. This is a 1930s Grimstead photograph. (Reproduced courtesy of the Metuchen-Edison Historical Society.)

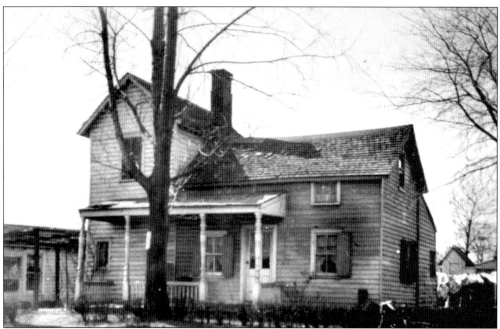

In 1936, Pat Higgins owned this house on the north side of Oak Tree Road. Note the outhouse and shed behind the house. Grimstead was the photographer. (Reproduced courtesy of the Metuchen-Edison Historical Society.)

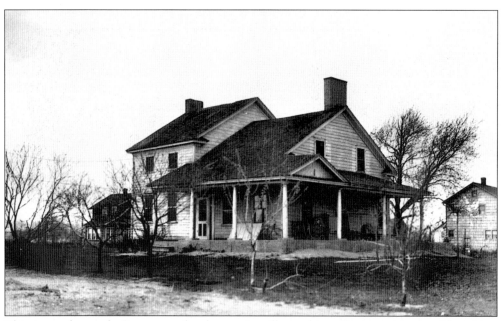

This is another early Samptown farmhouse. It still stands on Dumont Avenue. The oldest section of the house is presumably the section to the right, and main block of the house is on the left. When Grimstead photographed it in 1936, he noted that it was 100 years old. At that point, J. Stone owned the house. Note the newer houses behind and to the left of the building. (Reproduced courtesy of the Metuchen-Edison Historical Society.)

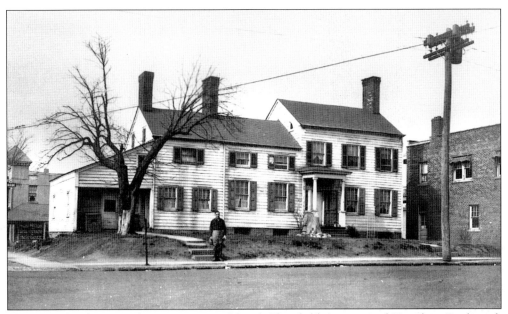

The Ryno farmhouse at the intersection of South Plainfield Avenue and Hamilton Boulevard, one of the oldest houses in town, contains sections that date from the 18th century. The 10-room house stood on a knoll that was later leveled. In the 1960s, a bank, which later became the senior-citizens center, was constructed on the spot. The photograph was taken in 1933. Lew Ryno is standing in front of the house. Like many vernacular farmhouses, it grew over time with additions and remodeling. (Reproduced courtesy of the Metuchen-Edison Historical Society.)

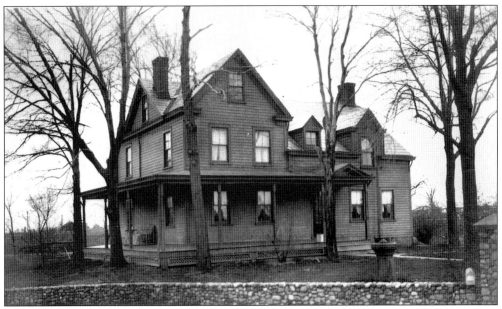

This fine Victorian building, the S. Manning house, once stood in what is today Holy Redeemer Cemetery. The stone wall in front of the house apparently posed a hazard to early motorists. After cars had repeatedly crashed into it, the wall was removed. J. Stone's house can be seen in the distance to the left. (Reproduced courtesy of the Metuchen-Edison Historical Society.)

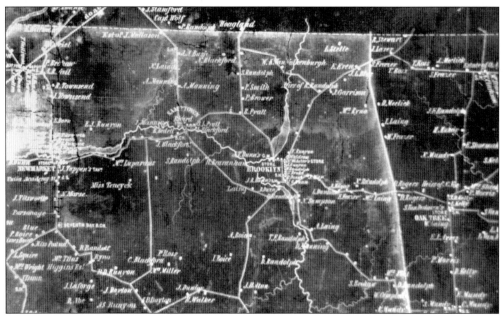

The J.W. Otley and J. Keiley 1850 *Map of Middlesex County* clearly shows the villages of Samptown and Brooklyn, which grew to be South Plainfield. A few years earlier, in 1838, Samptown had been described as having 12 dwellings, a tavern, a store, and a church, while New Brooklyn had 10 dwellings and 2 mills.

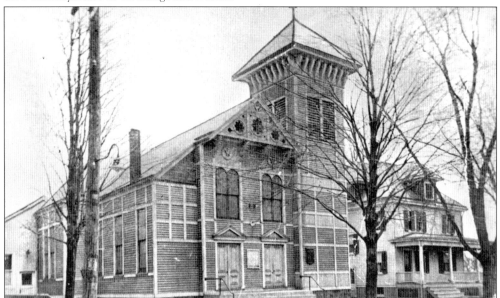

This photograph shows the Baptist church and parsonage in South Plainfield. This structure, located at the intersection of Church Street and Hamilton Boulevard, was the third church built by South Plainfield's Baptist congregation. Their first church, built in 1792, was located in the old Samptown, or Waterville, Cemetery on New Market Avenue. It was torn down, and a second church was constructed in the same location in 1834. That church burned in 1879. Shortly thereafter, the congregation moved from Samptown to New Brooklyn. In 1880, they erected this impressive building.

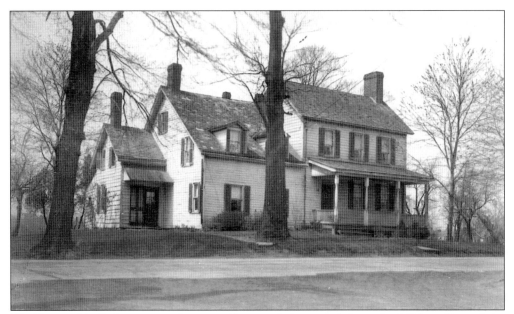

The Tappan-Faulks house, seen here in a Grimstead photograph from the 1930s, still stands on Maple Avenue. The house has lost its attractive porch and is located quite close to the road. The kitchen wing on the left of the house appears to be a modified Dutch cottage, and the right portion of the house is in the Federal style. In 1936, Grimstead noted that the owner was N. Webster and that the structure was 150 years old. (Reproduced courtesy of the Metuchen-Edison Historical Society.)

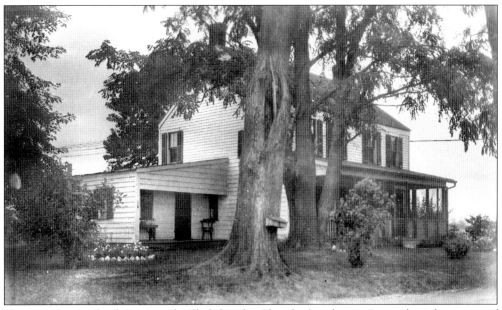

Photographer J. Lloyd Grimstead called this the Chamberlain house. It stood on the corner of Plainfield and Sampton Avenues, where the Quick Chek is located today. (Reproduced courtesy of the Metuchen-Edison Historical Society.)

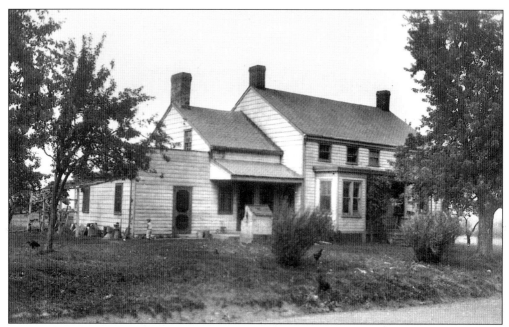

This early-20th-century photograph shows the Walker farm on Hamilton Boulevard. A grape arbor appears to be propped against the left side of the house, and a covered well is located in the front yard. (Reproduced courtesy of the Metuchen-Edison Historical Society.)

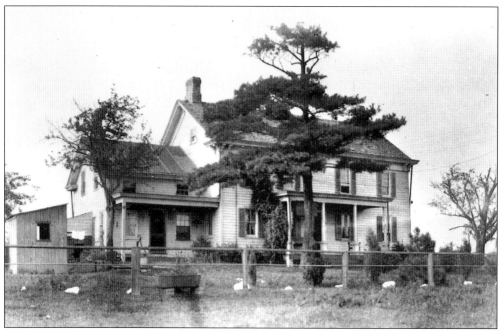

This is an early shot of the Geary farm on Plainfield Avenue. Today, it sports a very attractive porch. The structure, which is believed to date from the mid-19th century, will be demolished soon for a new development. When new, it must have been one of the most impressive farms in town. (Reproduced courtesy of the Metuchen-Edison Historical Society.)

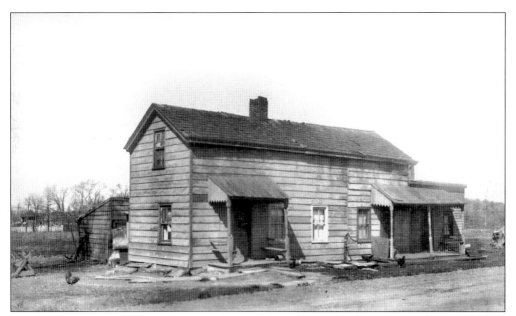

This ramshackle building stood on Hamilton Boulevard. Weather-beaten and worn, it probably dates from the mid-19th century. In 1936, it was owned by Pat Marr. The building is an excellent example of vernacular architecture. (Reproduced courtesy of the Metuchen-Edison Historical Society.)

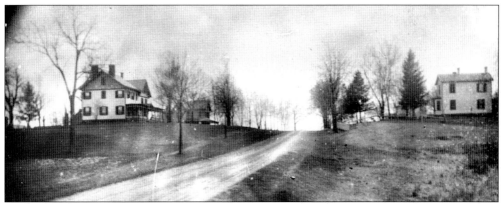

This is how Clinton Avenue looked at the end of the 19th century. In the 20th century, the house on the left was known as Stockoff's Farm. The Manning family originally owned it. The farm remained in operation into the 1970s. Hardly visible at the left of the photograph is a hay barracks. These were simple wooden shelters erected to protect hay from the weather. (Reproduced courtesy of the Plainfield Public Library, Paul Revere Collier Collection, donation of William T. Garrett.)

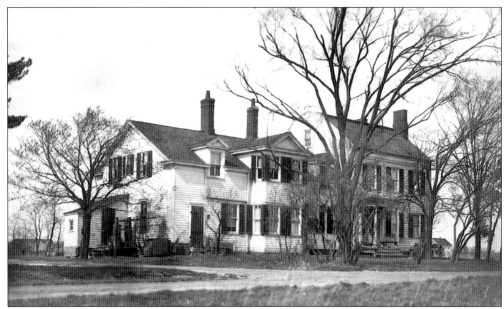

One of the finest farmhouses in South Plainfield was the Isaac Boice farm, which still stands on Montrose Avenue. Like many of the other farmhouses examined here, it clearly grew in stages. The side-hall-plan main block at the far right probably dates from 1808. (Reproduced courtesy of the Metuchen-Edison Historical Society.)

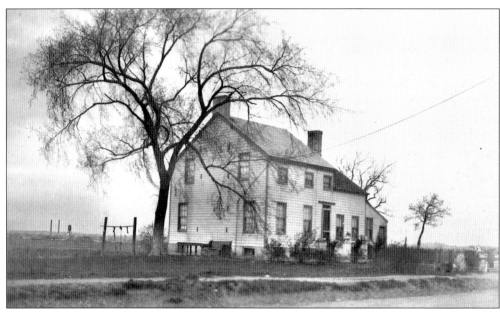

Grimstead called this Mrs. Brantingham's house. Located on Hillside Avenue, it still stands. Henry Brantingham was a sergeant in Company C of the 28th Regiment, New Jersey Volunteers. He was killed in action at Fredricksburg, Virginia, in December 1862. (Reproduced courtesy of the Metuchen-Edison Historical Society.)

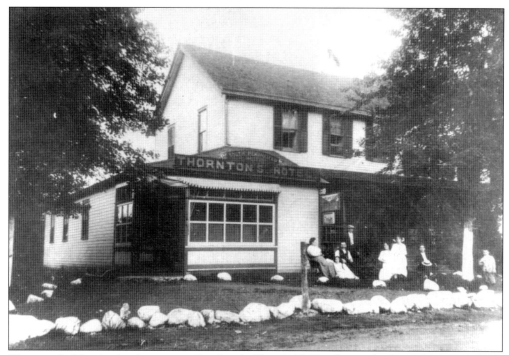

Thornton's Hotel, also known as the South Plainfield Hotel, stood where the Veterans of Foreign Wars Hall is located today. This scene shows it c. 1890.

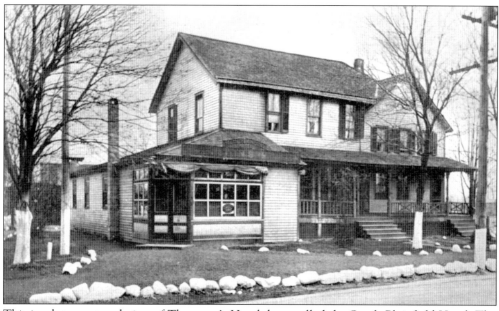

This is a later postcard view of Thornton's Hotel, here called the South Plainfield Hotel. The photograph probably dates from the first decade of the 20th century.

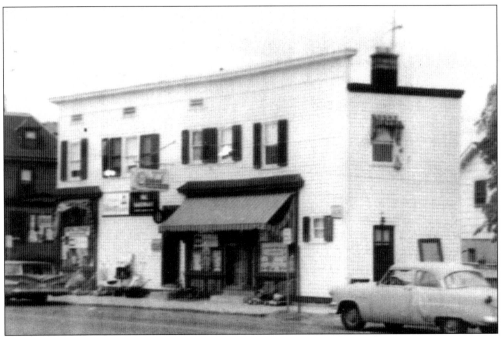

This is a photograph of Vail Hardware on the corner of South Plainfield Avenue and Front Street. The building was constructed by John Geary Sr. and once housed the post office. Since the early 20th century, Vail Hardware has been located here. Today, George Dencker owns it. His father purchased the building in 1956.

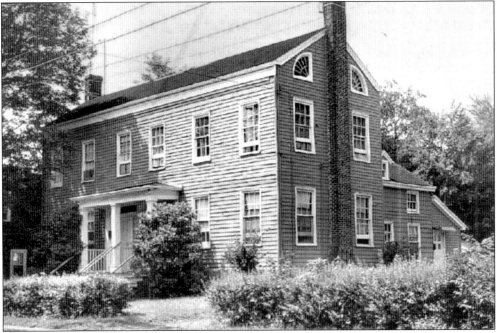

This fine Federal-style house was built c. 1836 by Furman and Jacob Fitz Randolph. The house stood on Front Street and was demolished in the 1980s. Little is known of its history, but it was one of the finest houses in town.

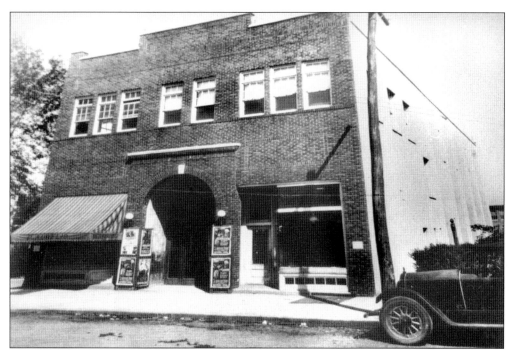

Joseph Siccardi built the Park Theater on South Plainfield Avenue in 1922. In the 1920s, the building was owned by the Sons of Italy Lodge and managed by the Liberty Theater of Plainfield. From 1933 to 1952, the DeSabato family owned it. The Park Theater seated 430 and was a popular spot to see movies up until the 1960s. The posters are for the films *The Kentucky Derby*, starring Reginald Denny, and *Up in the Air*.

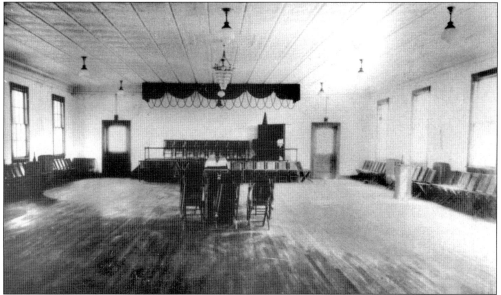

This is an unusual photograph of the Sons of Italy Club, located on the upper floor of the Park Theater. The chairs have been pushed up against the walls, perhaps to prepare for a dance. At the back of the room, where the photographer was standing, there was a large kitchen to prepare food for events.

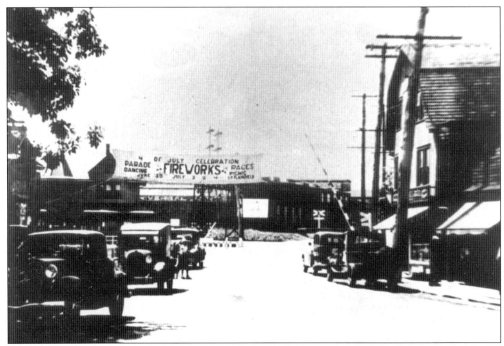

This early-20th century-photograph of Hamilton Boulevard is focused on the train station and the Spicer Factory. To the right is a general store and what would have been South Plainfield's main street.

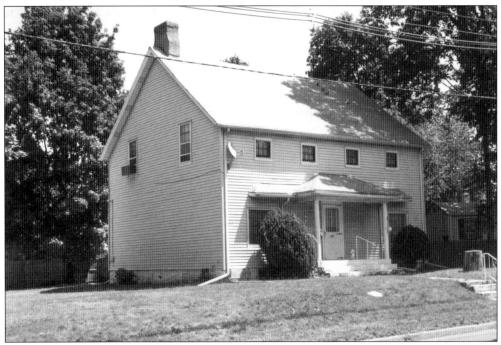

Hidden under the vinyl siding of the Laing farmhouse on New Market Avenue is an 18th-century-home. Like many of the early houses in town, this one stands on a low knoll and would have had a good view of the surrounding fields.

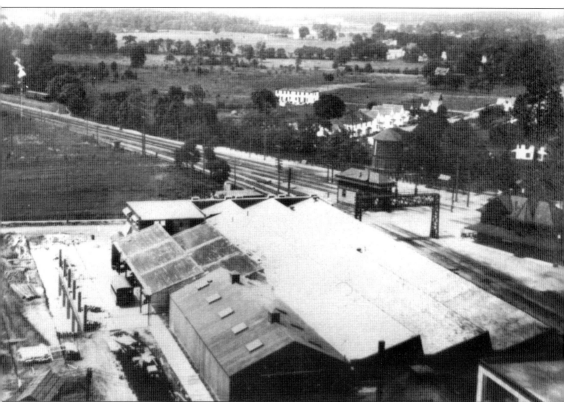

This is one of a series of aerial photographs taken *c.* 1914 showing South Plainfield from the newly constructed water tower of the Spicer plant. The photographs provide a unique panorama of early South Plainfield. Notice that the factory is under construction in the foreground. The train station and switching tower are visible in the center right of the photograph and downtown South Plainfield is visible to the right. The road running from right to left through the center of the photograph is Hamilton Boulevard.

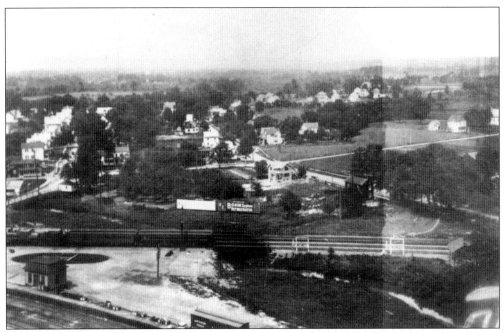

This aerial photograph was taken from the Spicer plant's tower c. 1914 showing downtown South Plainfield. The freight station is visible at the bottom left-hand corner of the photograph. The field in the center of the photograph is where Drug Fair is located today. At the far right side of the photograph a corner of the original Sacred Heart Church can be seen.

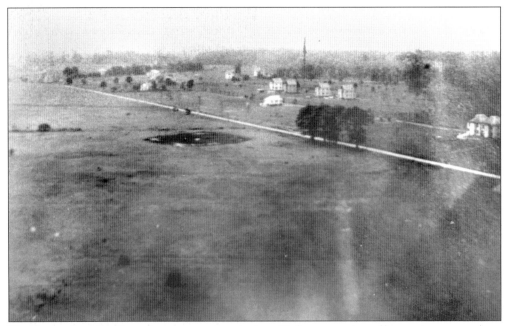

Here is another view from the same panoramic shot. Only a scattering of houses is present along New Market Avenue. Hamilton Boulevard is largely undeveloped. The dark spot near the center of the photograph is approximately where Our Lady of Czestochowa Church was constructed in 1943.

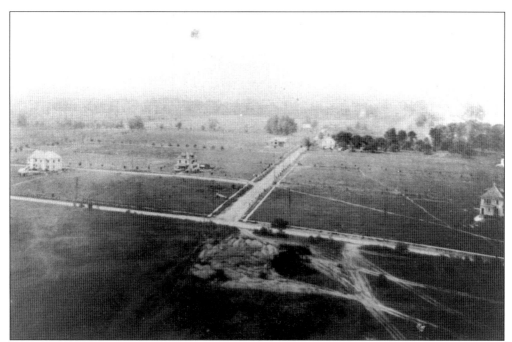

Seen here is the intersection of New Market Avenue and Hamilton Boulevard as it appeared c. 1914. Only a few houses have been constructed on the south side of town, the bulk of which remained open fields.

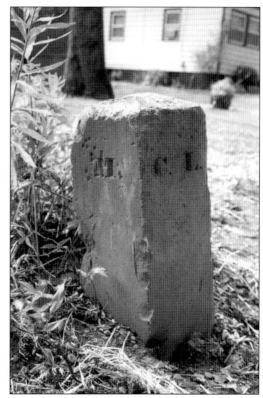

This small brownstone pillar stands in a residential neighborhood on Grant Avenue. It marked the boundary between Essex and Middlesex Counties and was erected before 1857. In that year, Union County was formed from Essex County.

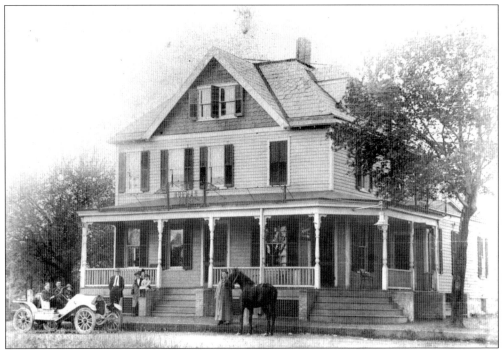

This is the Norman House, or William Norman's Hotel, a predecessor of Norman's Bar and Grill. The photograph shows the house and two popular forms of transportation in 1912. The Norman House stood on Hamilton Boulevard where Ralph's Italian Ices is located today.

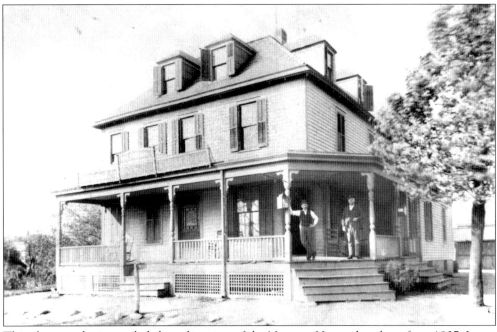

This photograph gives a slightly earlier view of the Norman House that dates from 1907. Later, the Lippett family, who had a children's clothing store in Plainfield, owned the house and sewed baseball uniforms here.

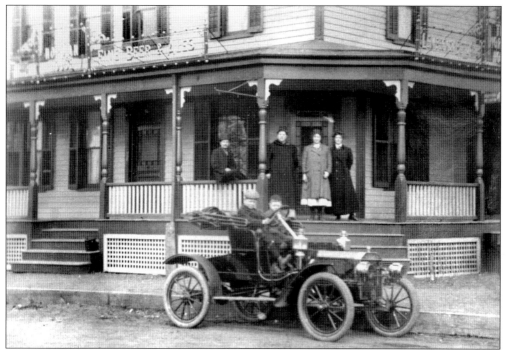

These two young boys appear to be trying out a new car. They are posed in front of the Norman House. Note the ornate sign advertising fine beer and ales.

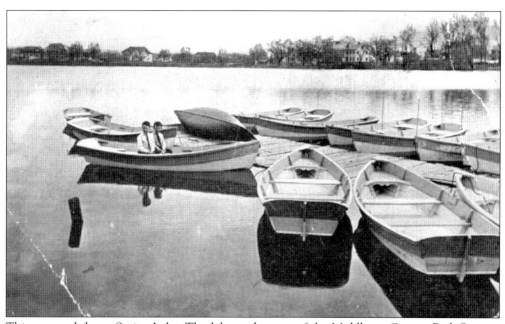

This postcard shows Spring Lake. The lake, today part of the Middlesex County Park System, is a major feature in the center of town. The photograph is titled "Boat Landing, Spring Lake, South Plainfield, NJ," and dates from the early 20th century. The lake was, in fact, the millpond for the gristmill.

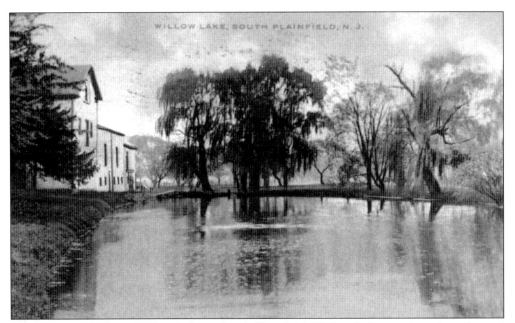

This photograph shows Willow Lake in South Plainfield. Willow Lake may have been located behind the current municipal building. This postcard, one of only a few that exist from the town, dates from the first decades of the 20th century.

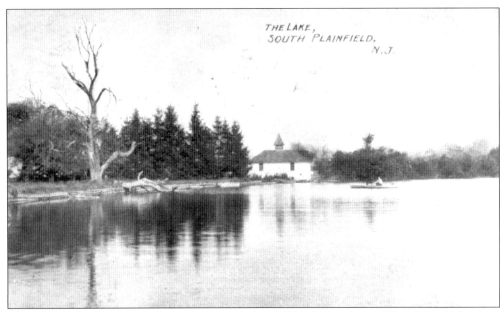

This postcard, showing a man rowing, is titled, "The Lake, South Plainfield, N.J." It is presumably Spring Lake, where there were a boathouse and rowboat rentals. The photograph dates from before 1920.

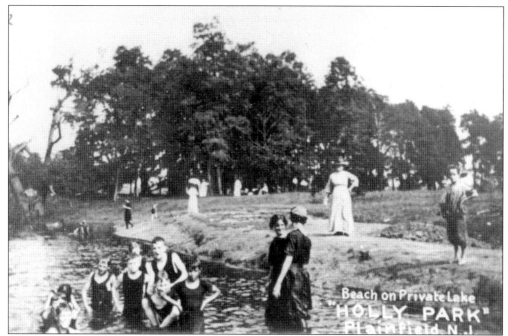

Although labeled "Beach on Private Lake 'Holly Park' Plainfield, N.J.," this photograph of a group of happy young swimmers was taken at Milton Mendell's Holly Park Resort off Park Avenue in South Plainfield. Holly Pond, the man-made lake shown here, was near the site of the current community pool. The postcard dates from the first decade of the 20th century.

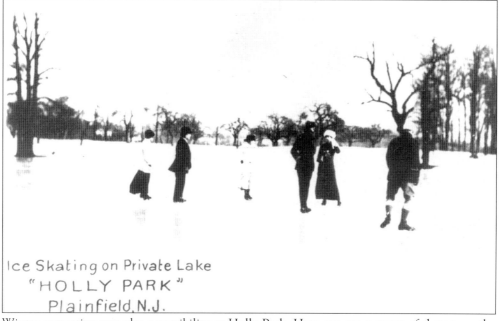

Winter recreation was also a possibility at Holly Park. Here, we see a group of skaters on the ice. Holly Pond was nine acres. In the winter of 1907, over 500 tons of ice was harvested there. Once again, although the postcard is labeled Plainfield, N.J., the location is South Plainfield.

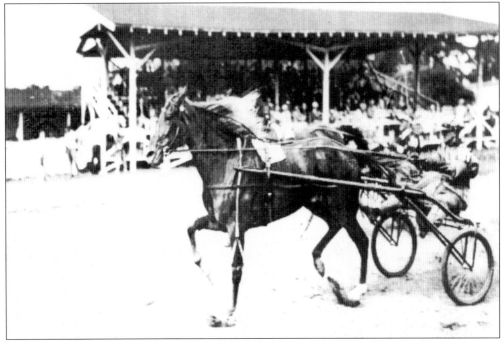

In the early 20th century, South Plainfield was home to two racetracks. The first, sometimes called Boro Park Race Track, was located between Tompkins and Franklin Avenues by the Maltby house. The other was located off Maple Avenue and was known as the Plainfield Driving Park. This photograph shows a sulky passing the grandstand at Boro Park Race Track.

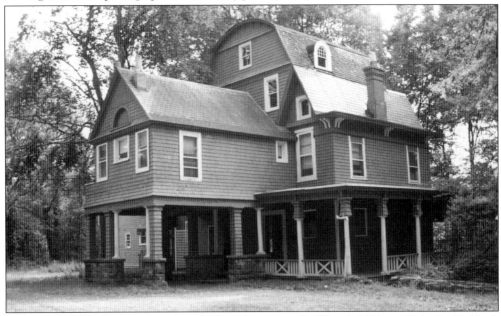

This is the Maltby house, which has also been known as the Plainfield Hunt Club, the Paddock Inn, Doc and Tim's, and TJ's Hideaway. An eclectic Victorian structure, it is somewhat out of place in rural South Plainfield. Stylistically, it might be considered an extension of Victorian Plainfield. Before it was built, a Blackford farmhouse stood on the property.

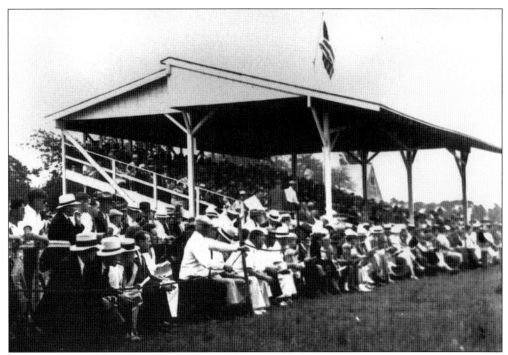

From the looks of the spectators it must be a close finish. Although today it is only a memory, Boro Park Race Track was once one of the best-known racecourses in the state. It closed in the 1930s.

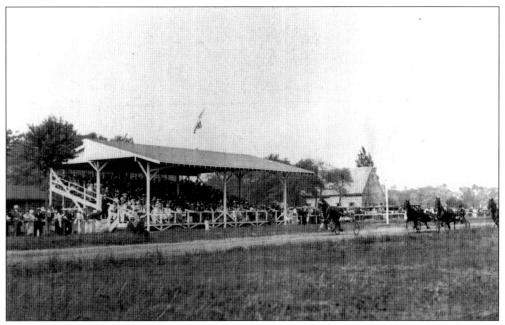

This action shot from the 1920s shows four sulkies in the home stretch. This may be the same race as the previous photograph. The Central Jersey Horsemen's Association operated the track, which had previously been known as the Plainfield Driving Club. The organization's letterhead claimed that they had the "Fastest 1/2-mile regulation track in the east."

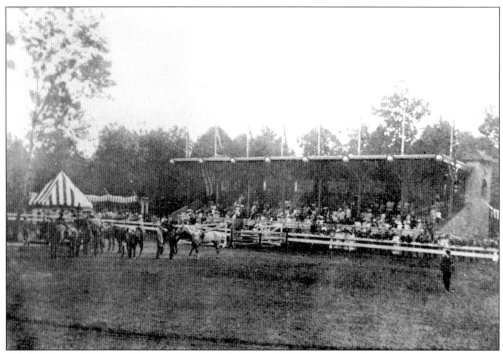

This photograph shows the grandstand at the Plainfield Driving Park, off of Park Avenue near East Crescent Parkway. Today, there is a medical building on this corner. In the 19th century, Tom Brantingham's Maple Tree Inn was located there.

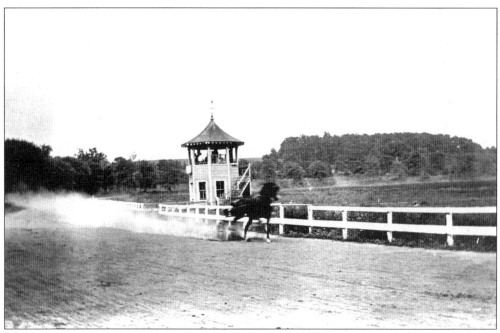

This is another early South Plainfield racetrack photograph. This photograph is believed to show the Plainfield Driving Park and dates from the 1890s. Notice the judging stand.

This c. 1914 photograph shows J.T. Castles's Ice Cream shop. This building still stands. Currently, it houses the South Plainfield Liquor Store on Hamilton Boulevard.

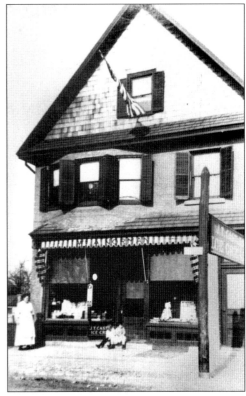

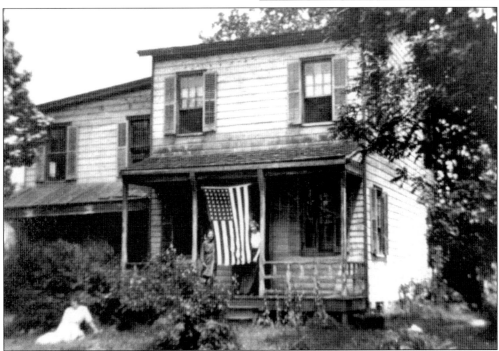

This patriotic scene is of Decoration Day in 1915 at the Soper house on Hamilton Boulevard. This house was recently torn down and a three-family home was erected on the site.

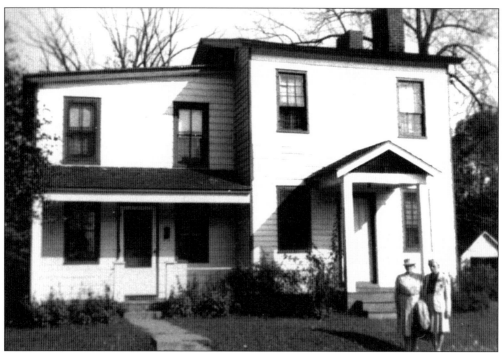

Seen here is a later shot, probably taken in the late 1950s, of the Soper house. Mildred Norman and Marjorie Bauer are posed out front.

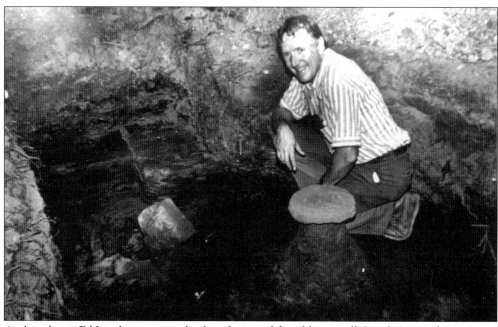

Archaeologist Ed Lenik excavates the foundation of the old gristmill. Lenik is crouching on top of the turbine that powered the mill. The Laing family built the first mill on the site in the 18th century. Variously known as the Dunham Mill, the Dunn Mill, and Randolph's Mill, this building was lost to fire in 1907. The site was partially excavated in 1986.

Two
Rural Life in Central Jersey

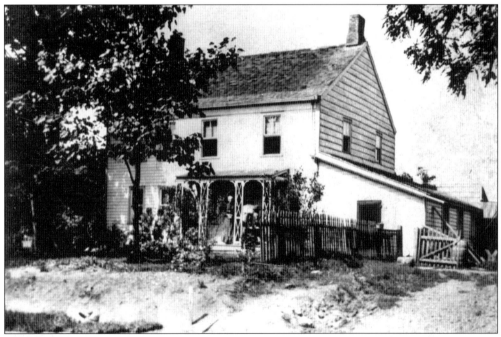

The Ten Eyck house at 1023 Maple Avenue is seen in this early 20th century photograph. The farm associated with this house once extended all the way to Park Avenue. The house is believed to have been constructed in the 1740s. Local folklore has it that Barzilla Randolph, from the roof of his barn, fired his gun at the British who were tearing down his fences. Another tale notes that a Hessian soldier was hanged on a tree behind the house.

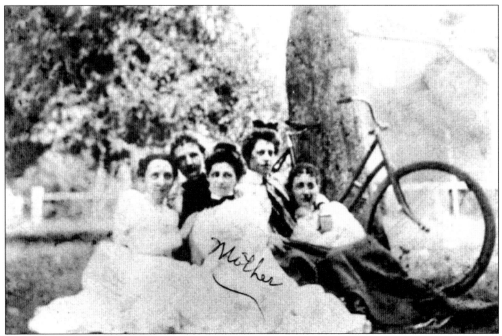

Here are some fashionable ladies at the Ten Eyck house, c. 1890. The women are, from left to right, Florence Vail, Margaret Ludlum, Lizzie Dalrymple Man, Flossie Compton, and Gertie Man.

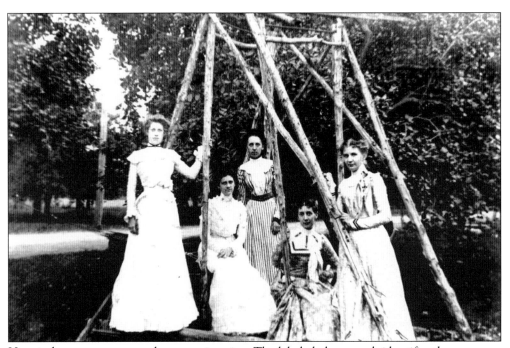

Here is the same group posed on a rustic swing. The labeled photograph identifies these women as Florence, Flossie, Gertie, Lizzie, and Florence.

This tintype photograph of Bethune Dunham (1828–1921) was taken in the 1870s. Dunham's house still stands on New Brunswick Road, near the Piscataway border. He is buried in Samptown Cemetery.

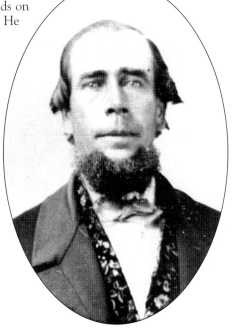

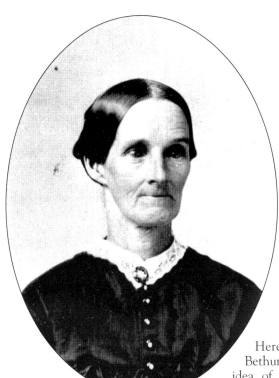

Here is Charity Dunham (1823–1912), Bethune's wife. This tintype photograph gives an idea of the fairly somber clothes, which were popular at the time.

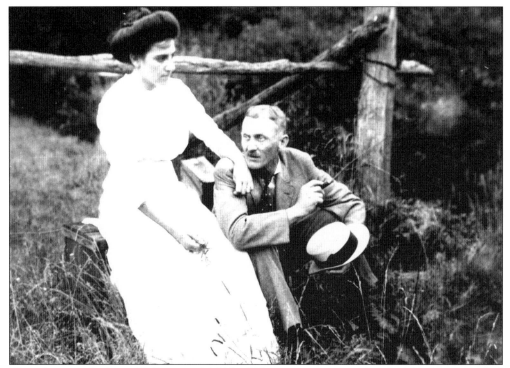

This photograph shows William and Mildred Norman in a relaxed pose. The Normans had extensive real-estate holdings in what would become South Plainfield in the late 19th century. William died on Christmas day in 1941.

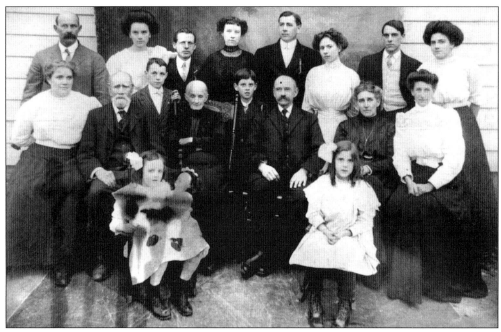

Bethune and Charity Dunham pose with their children and grandchildren. The photographer's backdrop is not quite big enough for all of them.

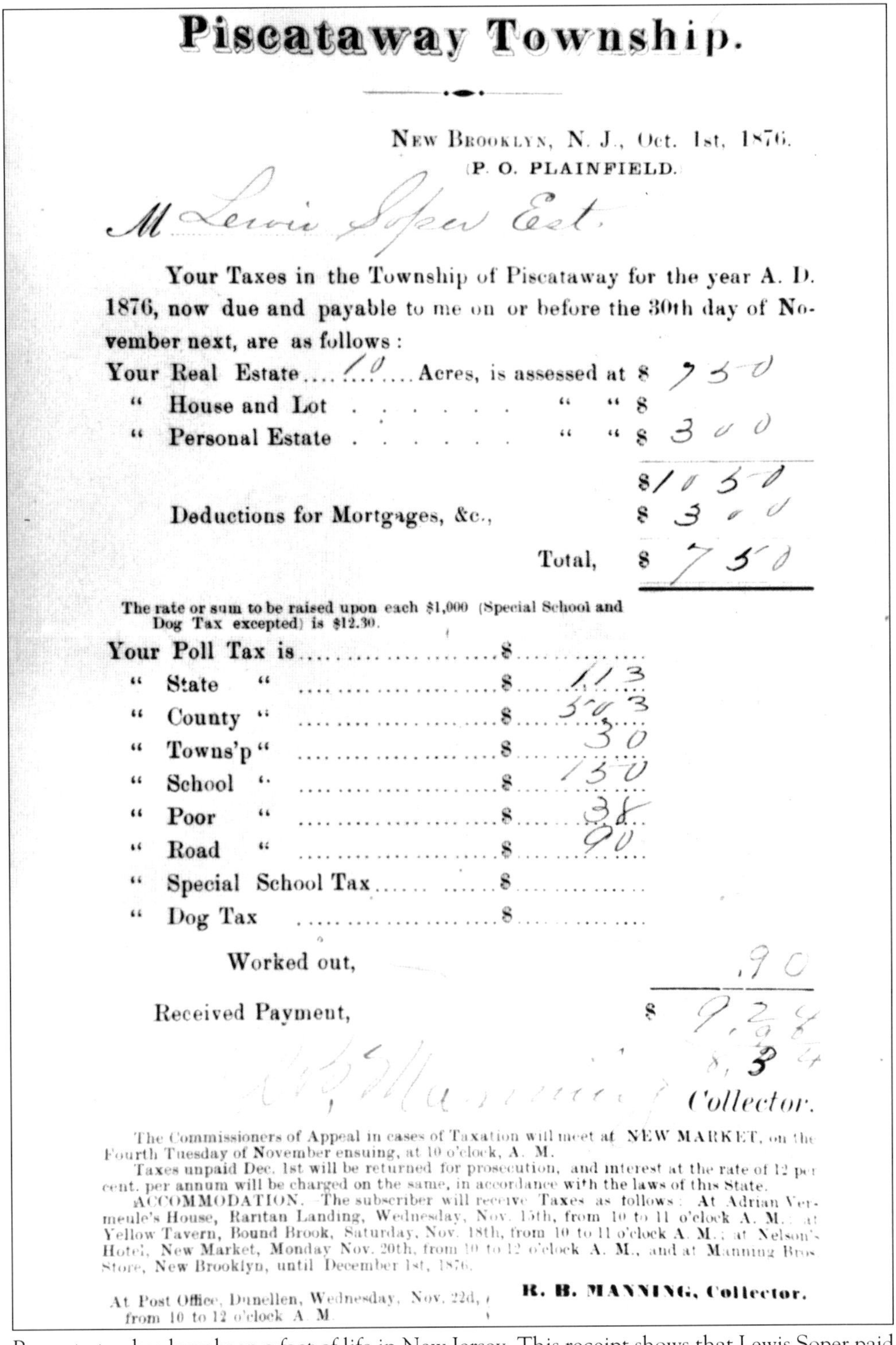

Piscataway Township.

New Brooklyn, N. J., Oct. 1st, 1876.
(P. O. Plainfield.)

M *Lewis Soper Est.*

Your Taxes in the Township of Piscataway for the year A. D. 1876, now due and payable to me on or before the 30th day of November next, are as follows:

Your Real Estate....*10*....Acres, is assessed at $ *7 5 0*
" House and Lot . . . . " " $
" Personal Estate . . . . " " $ *3 0 0*

$ *10 5 0*

Deductions for Mortgages, &c., $ *3 0 0*

Total, $ *7 5 0*

The rate or sum to be raised upon each $1,000 (Special School and Dog Tax excepted) is $12.30.

Your Poll Tax is .... $
" State " .... $ *1 13*
" County " .... $ *5 43*
" Towns'p " .... $ *30*
" School " .... $ *1 50*
" Poor " .... $ *38*
" Road " .... $ *90*
" Special School Tax ..... $
" Dog Tax .... $

Worked out, *.90*

Received Payment, $ *9.28*

R. B. Manning, Collector.

The Commissioners of Appeal in cases of Taxation will meet at NEW MARKET, on the Fourth Tuesday of November ensuing, at 10 o'clock, A. M.

Taxes unpaid Dec. 1st will be returned for prosecution, and interest at the rate of 12 per cent. per annum will be charged on the same, in accordance with the laws of this State.

ACCOMMODATION. The subscriber will receive Taxes as follows: At Adrian Vermeule's House, Raritan Landing, Wednesday, Nov. 15th, from 10 to 11 o'clock A. M.; at Yellow Tavern, Bound Brook, Saturday, Nov. 18th, from 10 to 11 o'clock A. M.; at Nelson's Hotel, New Market, Monday Nov. 20th, from 10 to 12 o'clock A. M., and at Manning Bros Store, New Brooklyn, until December 1st, 1876.

At Post Office, Dunellen, Wednesday, Nov. 22d, from 10 to 12 o'clock A M

R. B. MANNING, Collector.

Property tax has long been a fact of life in New Jersey. This receipt shows that Lewis Soper paid $7.50 in taxes on his personal and real estate in 1876. He owned 10 acres of land.

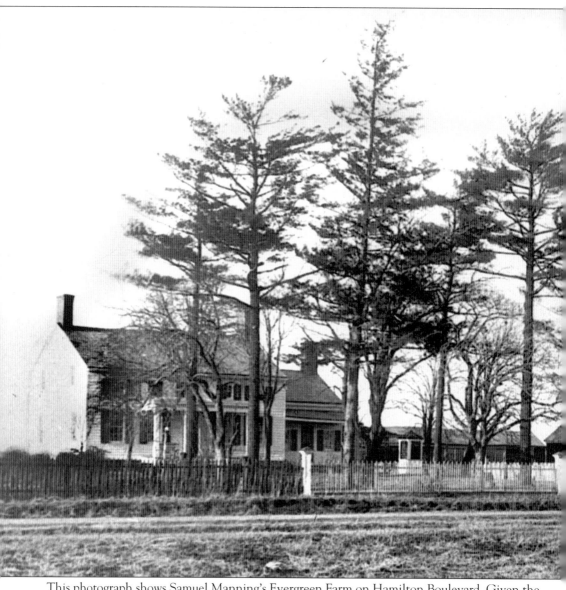

This photograph shows Samuel Manning's Evergreen Farm on Hamilton Boulevard. Given the towering trees, the farm appears to have been appropriately named. The farm operated into the

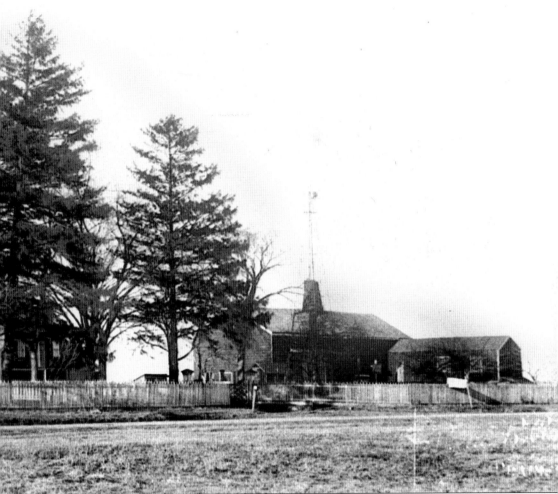

EVERGREEN FARM.
1-M FROM SO. PLFD. ST.

20th century and was located where HK Truck Services is now. Today, the area is densely developed and a passerby would hardly guess how pretty it once was.

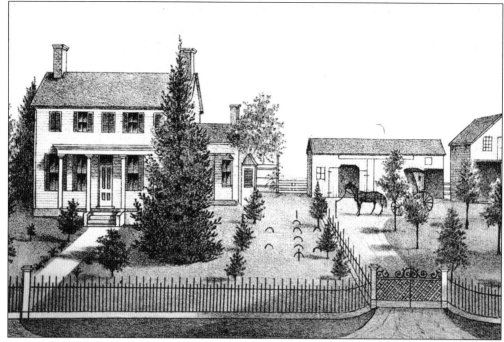

Samuel R. Manning's Evergreen Farm was the only South Plainfield farm grand enough to warrant inclusion in the Everts and Stewart 1876 *Atlas of Middlesex County*. This line drawing shows the farmhouse and an assortment of barns to its side.

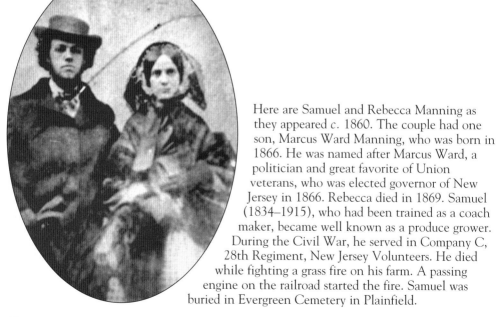

Here are Samuel and Rebecca Manning as they appeared *c.* 1860. The couple had one son, Marcus Ward Manning, who was born in 1866. He was named after Marcus Ward, a politician and great favorite of Union veterans, who was elected governor of New Jersey in 1866. Rebecca died in 1869. Samuel (1834–1915), who had been trained as a coach maker, became well known as a produce grower. During the Civil War, he served in Company C, 28th Regiment, New Jersey Volunteers. He died while fighting a grass fire on his farm. A passing engine on the railroad started the fire. Samuel was buried in Evergreen Cemetery in Plainfield.

This is an early-20th century photograph of Samuel R. Manning (center) with two of his grandsons, Everett Samuel Manning (left) and Samuel Manning.

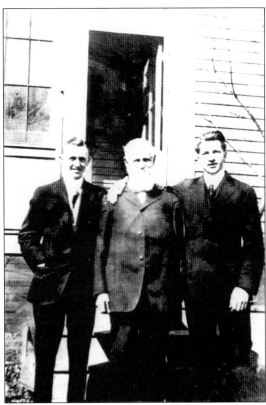

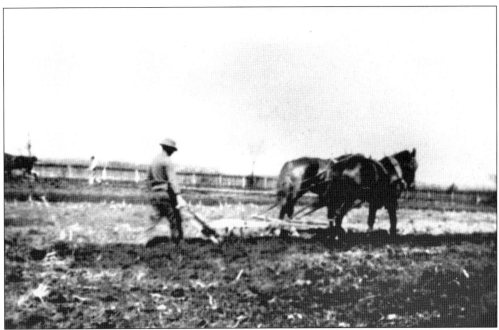

South Plainfield was known for its farms well into the 20th century. This scene from Evergreen Farm shows an individual plowing. Presumably a hired hand, he is identified simply as Thompson. In the background another man can be seen at work.

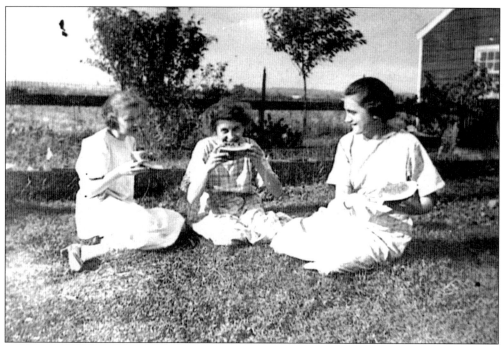
Three young ladies take time out for a watermelon snack on Evergreen Farm. Notice the sweeping vista in the background. Today, the site is filled with industrial buildings.

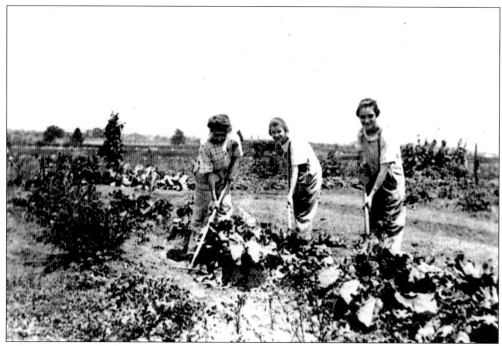
This picture titled "Farmettes" shows three happy young ladies hoeing the fields on the Manning farm.

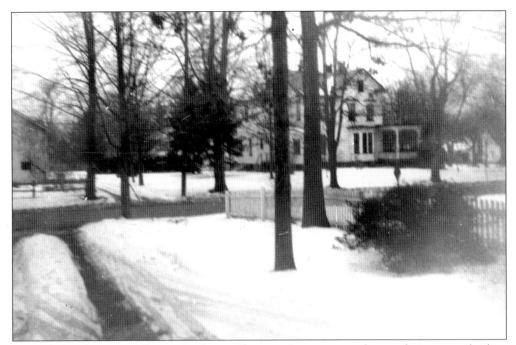

Several farmhouses still stand along Clinton Avenue in what today is a suburban neighborhood. This wintry scene from the collection of Bruce Ryno shows a farmhouse and a barn on the corner of Clinton and Tompkins Avenues.

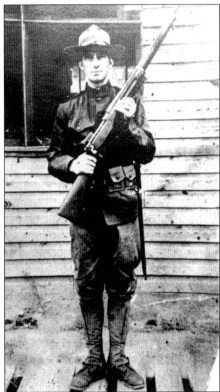

Robert Randolph was one of many young men from South Plainfield who served during World War I. He is seen here in his full uniform.

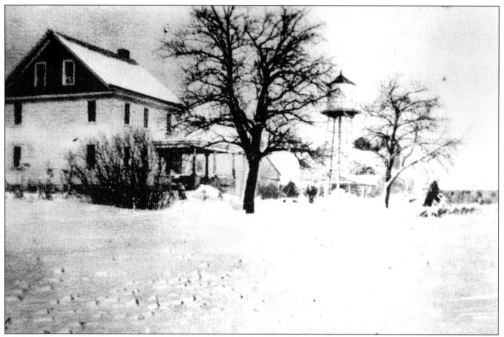

This snow-covered scene is Hadley farm before its transformation into Hadley Airfield. Owned by John R. Hadley, it was first employed as an airfield during World War I, when aviators would stop there en route to Washington D.C. The post office selected it as an airmail terminus in 1923 because of the level field and good flying weather.

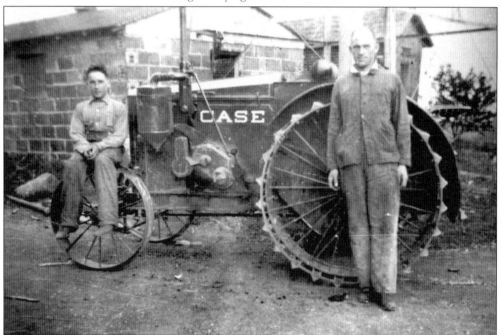

Two men pose by a tractor manufactured by the J.I. Case Company on the Hadley farm. Note the corncrib in the back right. The farm was owned by Benjamin Hadley and operated by his brother John.

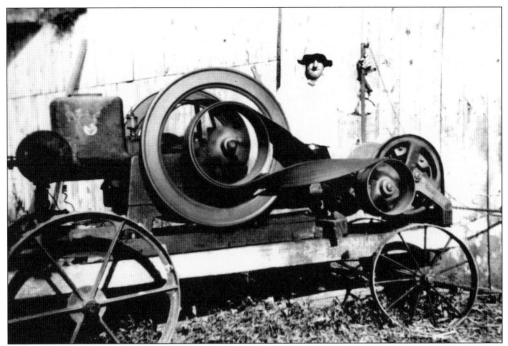

This is a single-cylinder gas engine at work on the Hadley farm c. 1914. The leather belts that transferred the power from the engine to various tools can be seen whirring away on the front of the machine. The belts posed a constant hazard to people working with these machines.

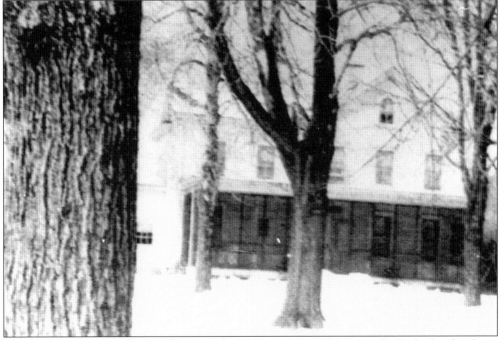

The Colucci farm, seen here, still graces Maple Avenue. In 1876, it was the Parks family's farm. In this photograph, it has a screened-in porch and appears to have a garage next to it. The house has been lovingly restored to an appearance similar to its 1870s character.

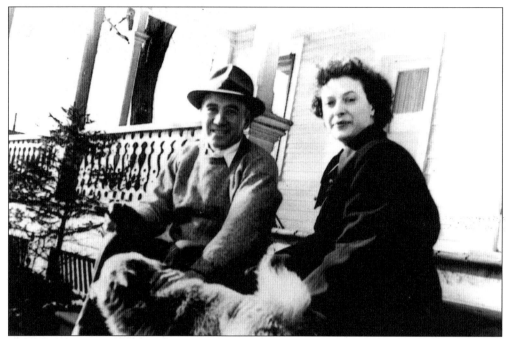

This is an informal view of the Coluccis on the porch of their house in the 1950s. Demetrio Colucci came to South Plainfield in 1915. He worked at both the Spicer plant and Harris Steel before purchasing the farm on Maple Avenue in 1942. Demetrio and his brother Bill owned a gas station on the southwest corner of Maple Avenue from 1930 to 1957. An Exxon station has replaced it.

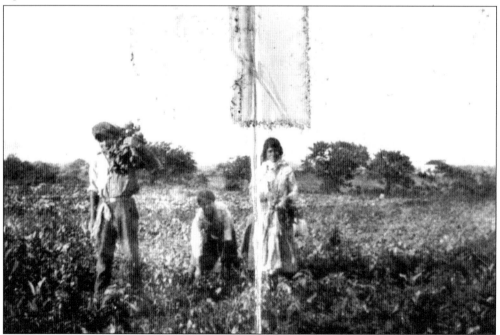

Harvest time on the Muglia's Hillside Avenue farm. In the 19th century, this was the Brantingham farm. The field appears quite productive in this early 20th century photograph.

This informal photograph was labeled in pencil, "The Muglia Orchestra." It dates from the 1920s or 1930s. The band includes a banjo, drum, and trumpet.

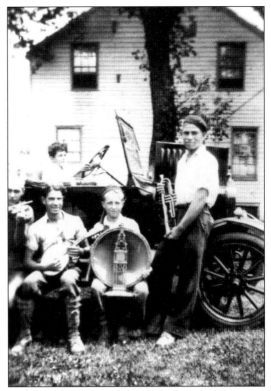

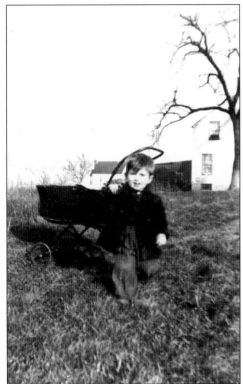

A young Robert Bengivenga approaches the photographer on the Muglia's Hillside Avenue farm. During the 20th century, the produce grown on the farm was sent to the Muglia's grocery store in Brooklyn.

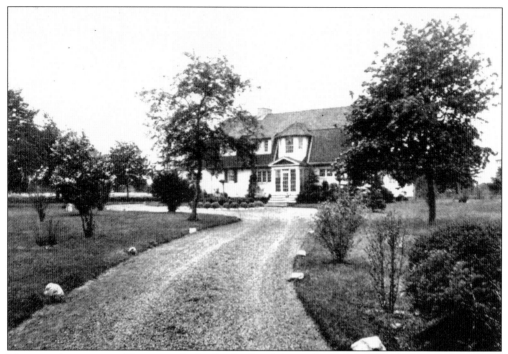

This is a front view of Longmead, the Linke family's residence. A fine example of Victorian architecture, it seems out of place among the farms and factories of turn-of-the-century South Plainfield. The photograph was taken in the 1920s.

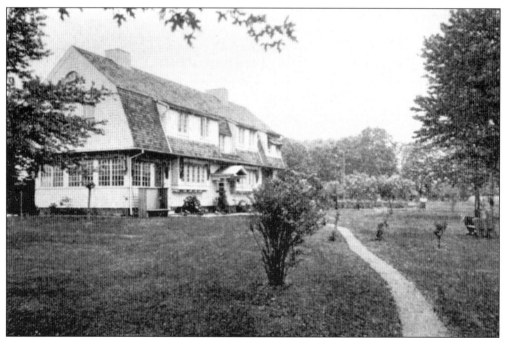

Longmead is seen from the rear. The house still stands on Linke Court, though the expansive lawns and winding driveway are now replaced by split-level and Cape Cod-style houses.

Three
TRANSFORMED BY THE RAILROAD

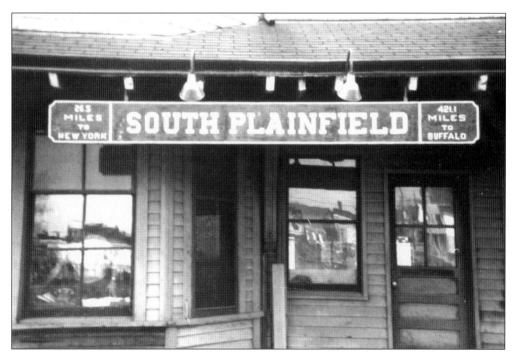

As the old railroad station sign points out, South Plainfield is located just 26.5 miles from New York and 421.1 miles from Buffalo. South Plainfield was almost entirely rural until the arrival of the Lehigh Valley Railroad in the 1870s.

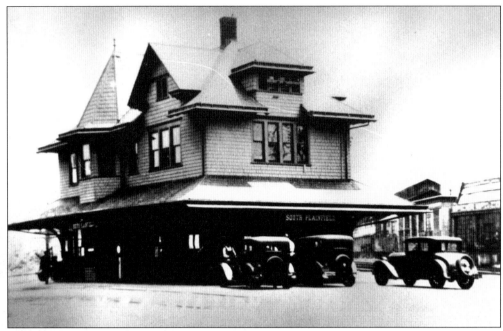

This photograph shows the Lehigh Valley Railroad's South Plainfield Station with the former Spicer plant in the background. This picture dates from the 1930s.

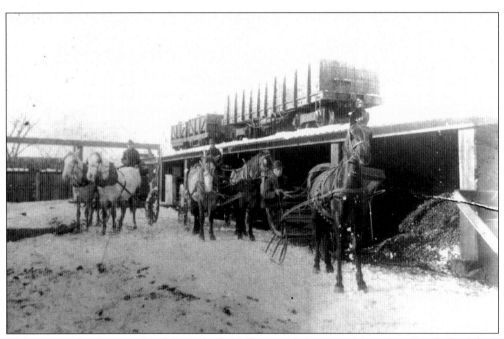

This is an early photograph of the Lehigh Valley's coal depot on Metuchen Road. Coal from Pennsylvania was brought here and stored prior to shipment to New York, Newark, and other cities. The trains could be run up on the trestle so that the coal could be dumped.

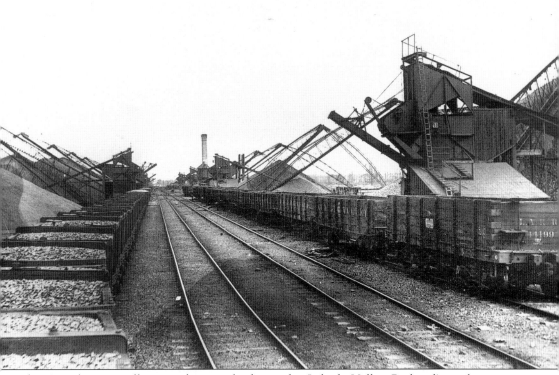

This Brinckmann collection photograph shows the Lehigh Valley Railroad's coal storage facility on the Perth Amboy Branch c. 1895. The depot was located between the Lehigh Valley main line and the Easton-Amboy line. It was largely automated, which allowed enormous quantities of coal to be moved with ease. Today, the coal moving equipment is gone but the switching yard remains.

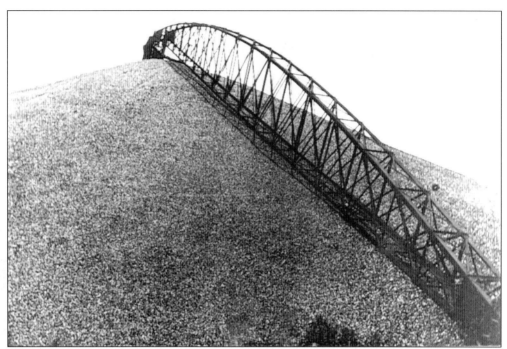

This is an enormous conveyor used to move coal at the storage facility on Metuchen Avenue. This photograph gives an idea of the scale of the operations there.

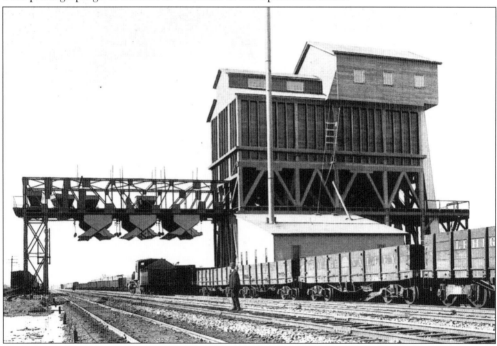

Seen here is the Lehigh Valley Railroad's main-line coaling station for locomotives. This structure burned on February 6, 1929. The building was 31 years old. The fire burned through the night despite a driving rainstorm. The loss was estimated at $150,000. When the structure collapsed, it closed all four tracks of the main line.

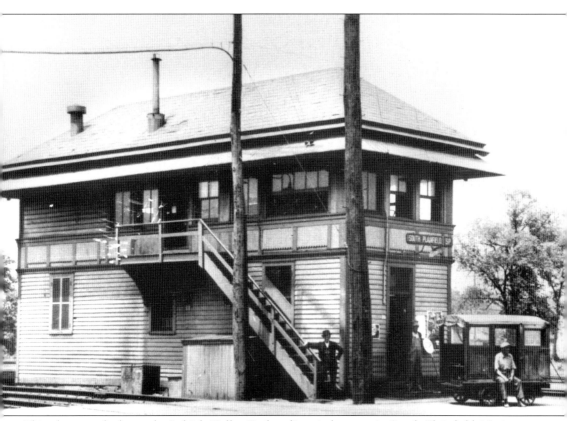

This photograph shows the Lehigh Valley Railroad's switch tower in South Plainfield. Notice the engineer standing by the side of the tower holding a stop sign and the man, perhaps a porter, resting on a luggage cart. Mike Morgan is shown on the stairs of the tower. The Lehigh Valley's main line and the Amboy branch split in South Plainfield, hence the need for the tower. The photograph dates from 1934.

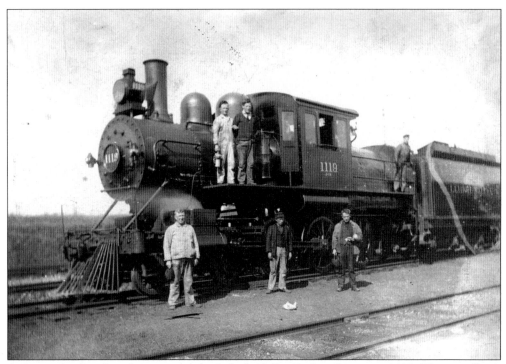

A group of railroad workers pose by the Lehigh Valley Railroad's engine 1119. The camelback locomotive appears to be a F-3 or N-1 engine. They were constructed between 1903 and 1910 and used until the end of the 1920s.

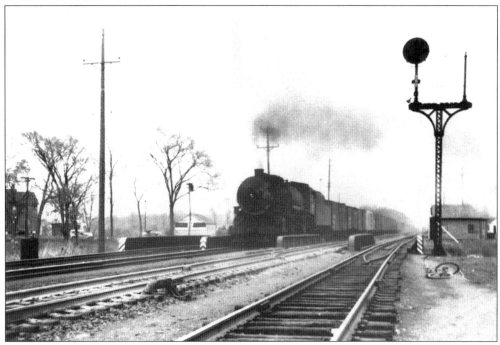

A fast freight barrels through town. This photograph, taken by John Brinckmann, probably dates from the 1940s. A bicycle has been hastily abandoned by the side of the tracks.

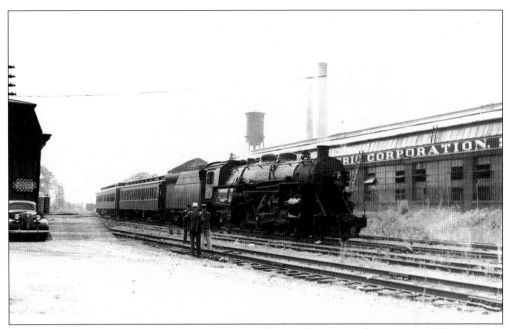

This is a Brinckmann photograph of Lehigh Valley Railroad president A.N. Williams's train arriving in South Plainfield on the Perth Amboy Branch for an inspection tour in 1939. Note the Cornell Dubilier plant in the background. To the left of the train, notice the building with the mansard roof. It was the freight station and may have been used as a passenger station before the later one was constructed.

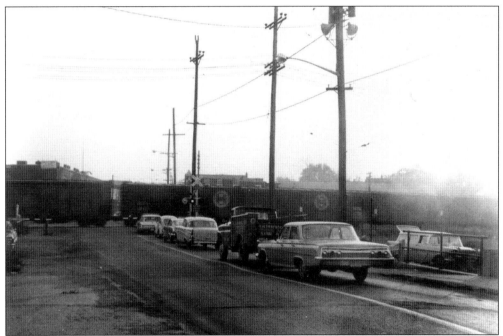

Until the construction of the Hamilton Boulevard overpass, waiting for trains was a fact of life for South Plainfielders. The tracks effectively cut the town in two. In fact, a second firehouse was built on the south side of town so that rescue vehicles would not have to wait for passing trains.

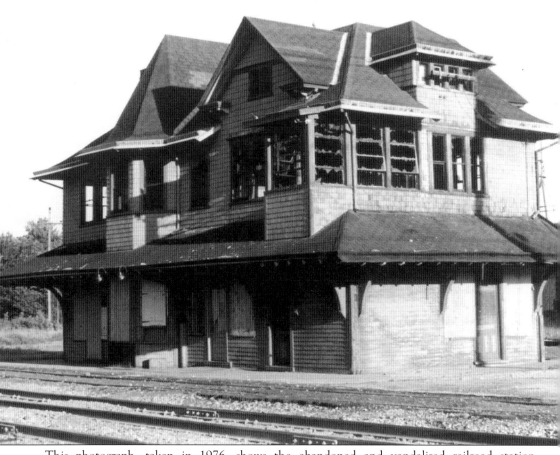

This photograph, taken in 1976, shows the abandoned and vandalized railroad station, constructed in 1895, shortly before its destruction. The last passenger service was in 1959. The building was razed on February 3, 1977. Developer Robert Bengivenga later constructed a replica on South Plainfield Avenue. It houses an attorney's office, an accountant, and a developer.

Four
INDUSTRY BUILDS SOUTH PLAINFIELD

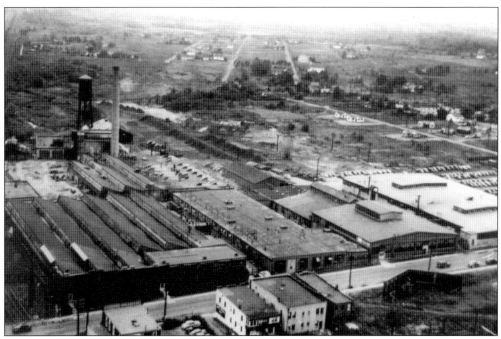

This 1930s photograph shows an aerial view of the Spicer Manufacturing Company plant, later Cornell Dubilier Electric Corporation. Hamilton Boulevard is at the bottom of the photograph. The fields to the east of the factory are starting to become filled with houses.

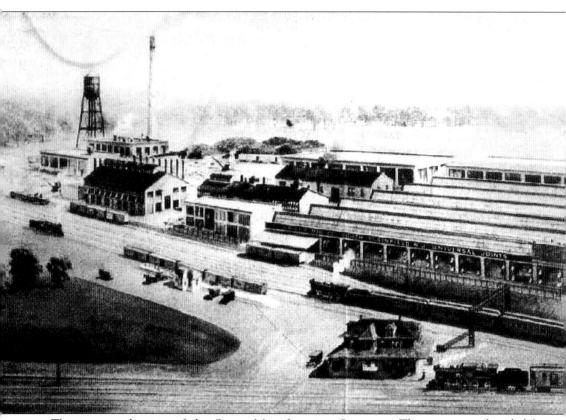

This is an early view of the Spicer Manufacturing Company. The company, founded by Clarence Spicer, moved to South Plainfield from Plainfield in 1910. Spicer manufactured universal joints and drive shafts for early trucks and automobiles. In 1914, Charles Dana bought into the successful company. Spicer was a paternalistic organization that built subsidized housing, had a nonprofit cafeteria, and contributed greatly to the development of South Plainfield. The company moved to Ohio in 1930. Today, the Dana Corporation remains a leader in the manufacture of automotive parts. Notice the railroad station at the bottom of the illustration.

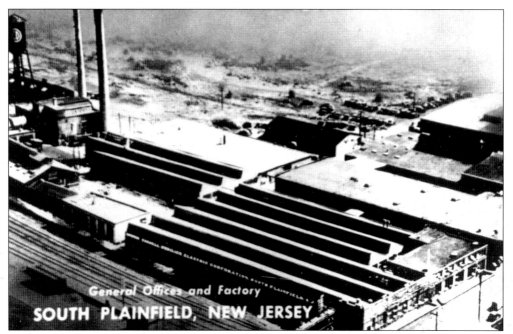

The Cornell-Dubilier Corporation manufactured condensers for radios and televisions as well as other electronic equipment in what had been the Spicer plant. For many years, it was the largest manufacturer in the borough and employed about 2,000 workers.

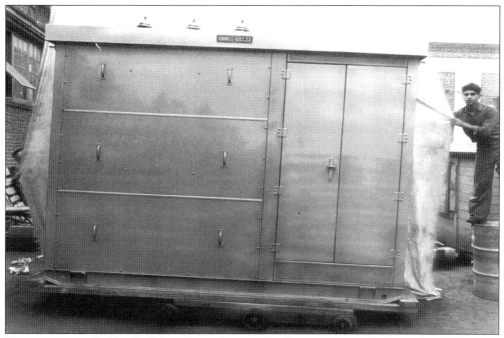

Two young men hold a backdrop for a photograph of a large piece of electrical equipment at the Cornell Dubilier plant. This is a Paul Collier photograph and may have been taken for insurance purposes. (Reproduced courtesy of the Plainfield Public Library, Paul Revere Collier Collection, donation of William T. Garrett.)

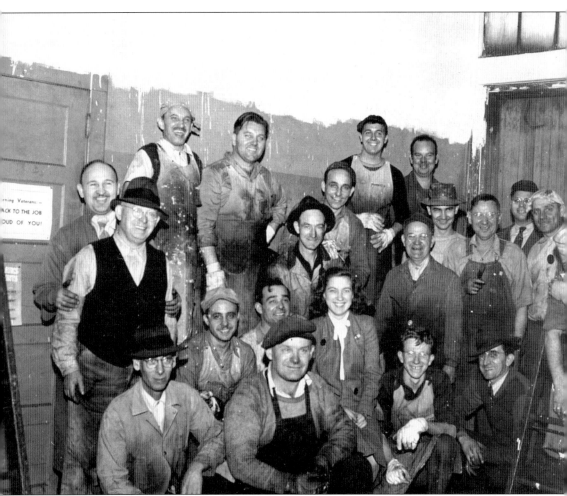

This is an informal shot of some happy machine shop employees at Cornell Dubilier taken in 1946. Notice the sign on the wall that reads, "Returning Veterans: Back to the Job, Proud of You!" Individuals in the photograph include Sammy Blum, Matty Brodzik, Ted Ferrante, Henry Ingraham, Frank Paycik, Benny Silver, Jim Browne, Charlie Galls, Charles Boseker, Walter Pyak, Walter Seifert, Herman Goldhammer, Arthur, Peter Penznik, Dom Agoista, Bill Kovack, Mary Mazepa, Carl Seamans, Frank Hudzik, Joe Bartog, and Jim Soper. (Courtesy of Mary Mazepa, South Plainfield Historical Society collection.)

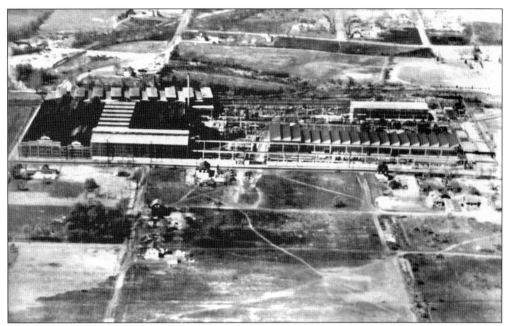

This photograph of the Harris Steel plant, taken in the 1930s, shows the earliest section of the gargantuan factory. Harris purchased the old Blackford farm and constructed the plant in 1915. Note the original alignment of New Brunswick Road as a shadow in the fields below the factory. During the plant's construction, the road was realigned to the west of the factory. The abutments for Holton's Bridge, which spanned the Bound Brook before the realignment, still stand. (Reproduced courtesy of Harris Steel.)

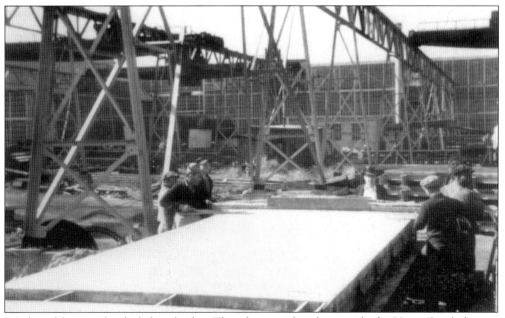

Workers fabricate the deck for a bridge. This photograph, taken inside the Harris Steel plant in the 1950s, illustrates the type of work performed there. The men appear to be smoothing the concrete surface of the deck. (Reproduced courtesy of Harris Steel.)

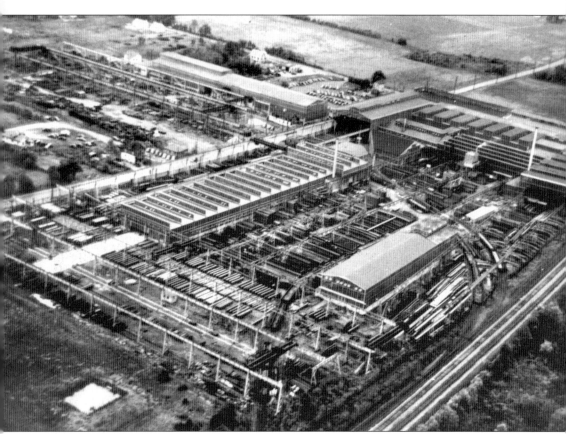

This is a 1950s photograph of the Harris Steel plant. Note the expansion of the plant to the south of New Market Road. During World War II, the factory manufactured landing craft. At its height, about 400 men were employed at the complex. Easily accessible by rail and highway, the plant has fabricated the steel work for many noteworthy structures, including the Betsy Ross Bridge, Verrazano-Narrows Bridge, and Newark Airport. (Courtesy of the South Plainfield Public Library.)

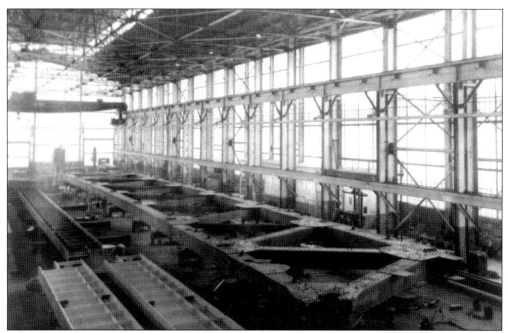

A view inside the Harris shops shows the massive framework the company made for the Port Authority's Manhattan bus terminal. (Reproduced courtesy of Harris Steel.)

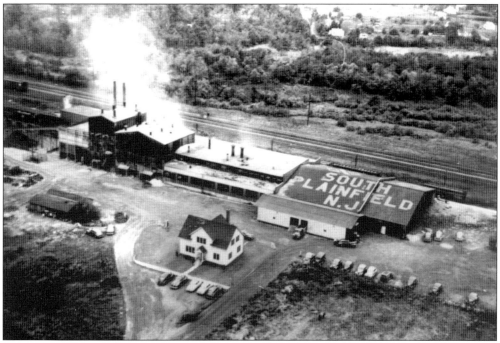

This aerial photograph shows the American Rock Wool Company's factory. This was one of several factories formerly located along the Lehigh Valley's main line through South Plainfield. It was built in 1936. The company manufactured home insulation products from furnace slag. At its height it employed 105 workers. (Reproduced courtesy of the South Plainfield Public Library.)

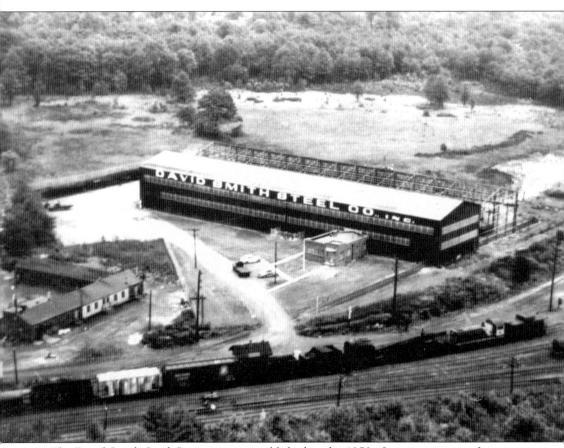

The David Smith Steel Company was established in the 1950s. It was not a manufacturing site but rather a distributor of structural steel, sheet, and bar stock. It employed about 60 workers and was located on Metuchen Road. Today, the site is vacant. (Reproduced courtesy of the South Plainfield Public Library.)

This is a view of the Middlesex Water Company's pumping station on Park Avenue. The smokestacks were constructed in 1916 and 1926, respectively. The smokestacks stood 125 feet high. This plant stopped operation in 1965, and the stacks were demolished in 1967. Notice the enormous pile of coal to the right that was used to fire the machinery in the pump house. Newer, more modern pumping facilities were later constructed on the site.

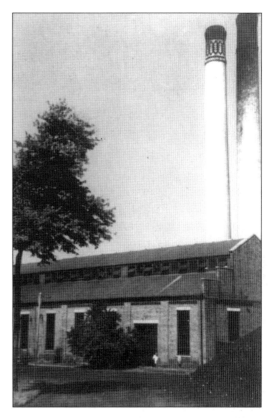

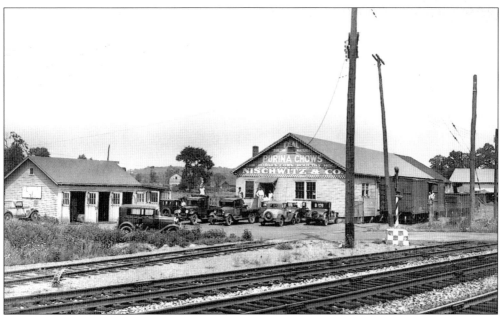

Nischwitz and Company, a feed and supply store, has long been a landmark in the center of town. This Grimstead photograph, taken in the 1930s, is an antique-car buff's dream. (Reproduced courtesy of the Metuchen-Edison Historical Society.)

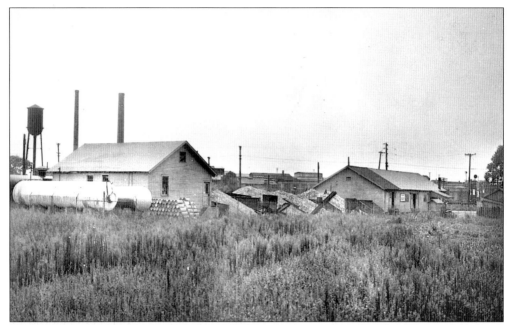

This is another 1930s photograph of the Nischwitz store on Metuchen Road. This view shows the well-stocked supply yard. Notice the piles of coal. The tracks of the Lehigh Valley Railroad are in the foreground. (Reproduced courtesy of the Metuchen-Edison Historical Society.)

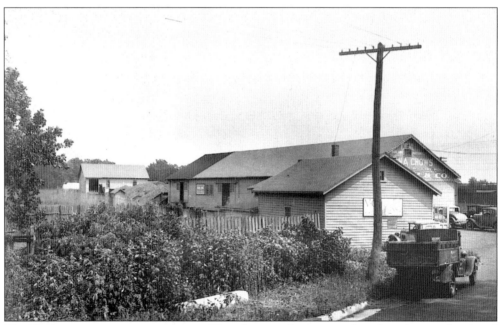

The Nischwitz store is seen once more. This photograph gives an idea of just how undeveloped downtown South Plainfield was in the 1920s. Note the early model dump truck parked by the very crooked telephone pole. (Reproduced courtesy of the Metuchen-Edison Historical Society.)

Five
HADLEY AIRFIELD

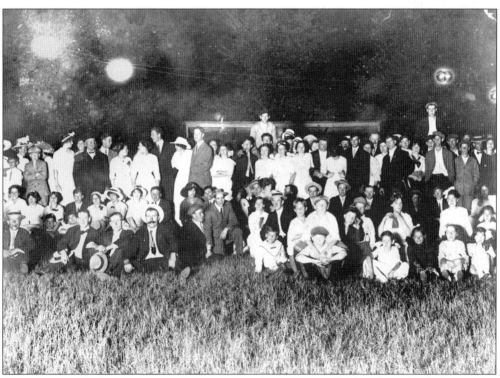

This photograph shows the crowd that gathered to witness the first transcontinental night airmail flight. Pilot Dean C. Smith took off from Hadley Field in a DH-4 on the first leg of the run. His destination was Cleveland, where the mail would be transferred to another flight. The flight took place on July 1, 1925. Over 15,000 people came out to witness the event. Smith crashed about 12 miles from Cleveland, but both he and the mail survived and eventually reached their destination.

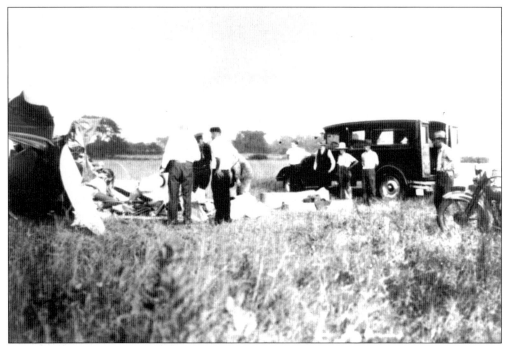

At an early crash at Hadley Field, the airplane, made of wood and canvas, is a total loss. The black station wagon in the background may be a hearse. Note the motorcycle to the right.

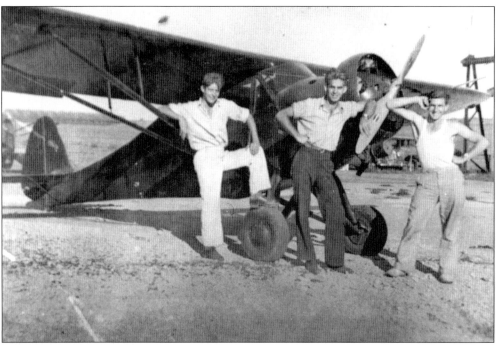

Seen here are would-be barnstormers at Hadley Airport in 1934. The young men are, from left to right, John Allen, Hank Allen, and Pete Reilly. The airplane is a Monocoupe, a popular high-performance small airplane.

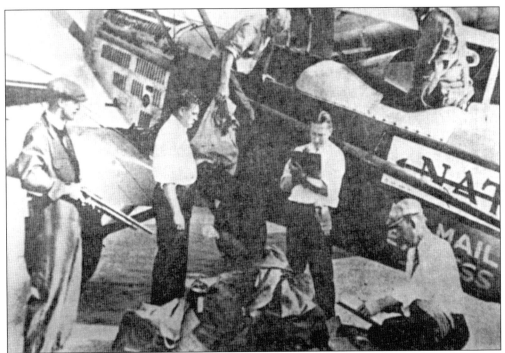

The mail must go through, and the armed gentleman with the shotgun will make sure of that. This 1920s photograph shows a mail airplane being loaded at Hadley Field. Although the field was located in South Plainfield, events occurring there were often reported as taking place in New Brunswick, the nearest city. Airmail sent through Hadley was postmarked New Brunswick.

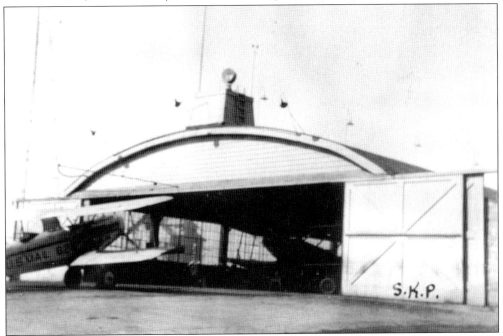

This is one of the hangers at Hadley Field prior to 1929. Notice that the airplane, a Douglas M-1, is marked "US MAIL."

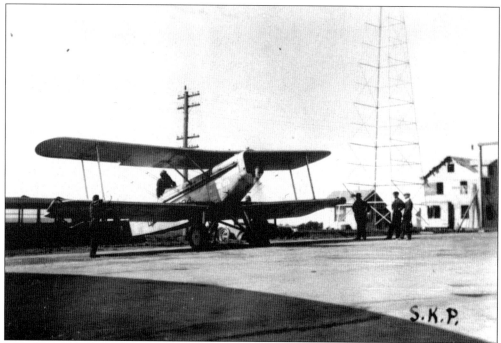

This airplane is preparing to depart for points west from Hadley Field with the mail. The propeller is turning and the pilot is slipping into the cockpit.

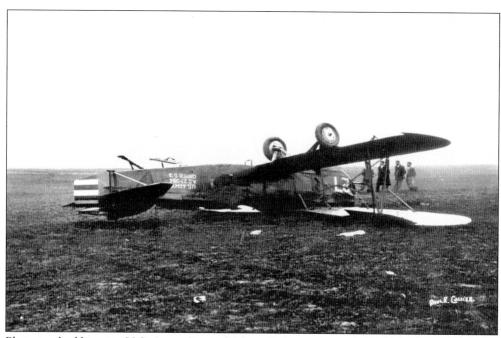

Photographed here is a U.S. Army Curtiss biplane that made a rough landing. Notice the wide-open vistas in the background. Today, this is one of the most densely developed portions of South Plainfield. The photograph dates from the 1920s. (Reproduced courtesy of the Plainfield Public Library, Paul Revere Collier Collection, donation of William T. Garrett.)

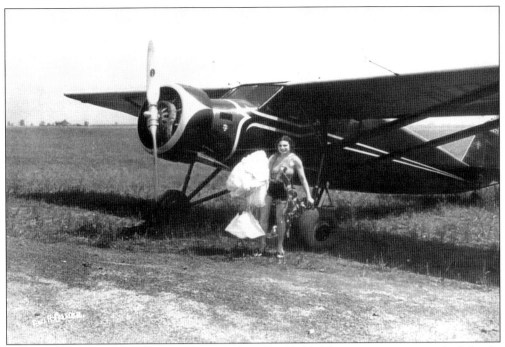

Barnstormers and aerial acrobats frequented Hadley Field. This young woman in high heels, whom we know only as Sue, performed at the field. (Reproduced courtesy of the Plainfield Public Library, Paul Revere Collier Collection, donation of William T. Garrett.)

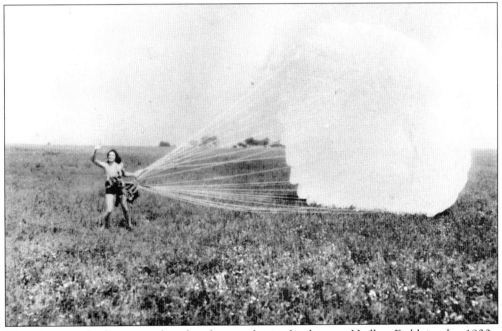

This photograph shows another female parachutist landing at Hadley Field in the 1920s. Unfortunately, her name is unknown. Other performances included wing walkers, upside-down flying, racing, and nosediving.

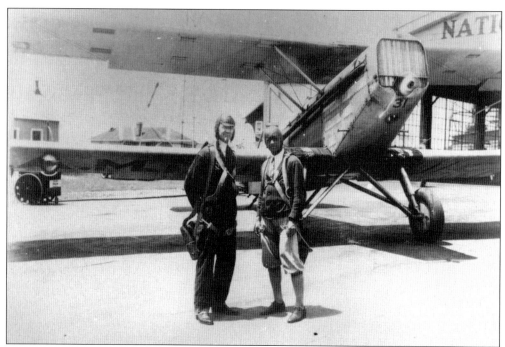

This photograph shows a U.S. Mail Douglas M-1 airplane. Notice the large landing lights on the wing tips. They were a necessity, as early airfields were not lighted. The picture dates from the mid-1920s. Airplanes like this one were flown by some of the first airmail pioneers.

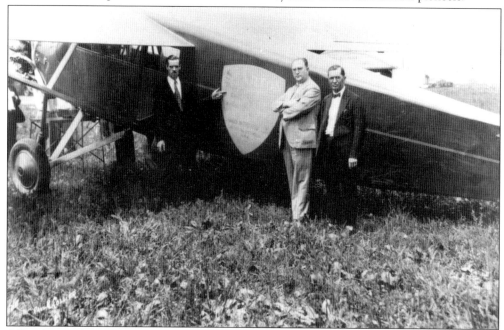

Officials posed with a Curtiss-Wright Robin, a very rare three-seat airplane. Douglas "Wrong Way" Corrigan accidentally flew one of these from Long Island to Ireland in 1938. He claimed that he had wanted to fly to Los Angeles but had compass trouble. These gentlemen appear far too serious for that sort of mistake.

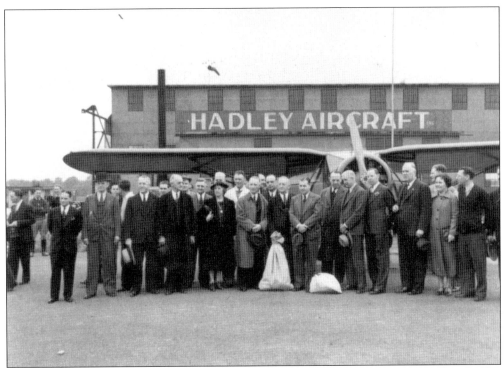

A group of dignitaries at Hadley Field posed with an airplane and two sacks of mail. The photograph was probably taken during airmail week in 1937. The airplane is a Fairchild Model 24.

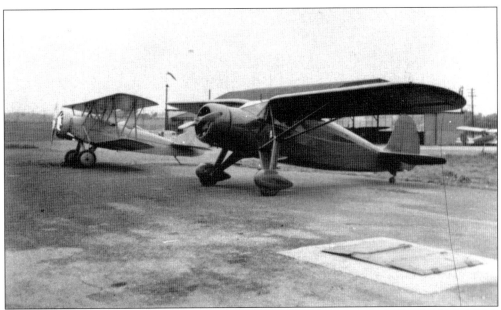

The airplane in the background is a Travel Air. In the foreground we see a Fairchild Model 24. They were built from 1932 to 1947. The design was the work of Raymond Loewy, who is famous for designing the Coke bottle.

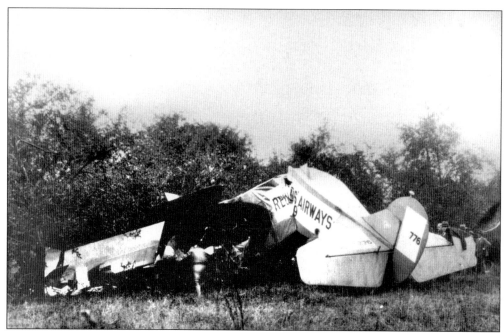

Here is yet another crash at Hadley Field. The airplane is a Fokker F-7 from Reynolds' Airways, which crashed on September 17, 1927, with seven fatalities. Early aviation was a hazardous business.

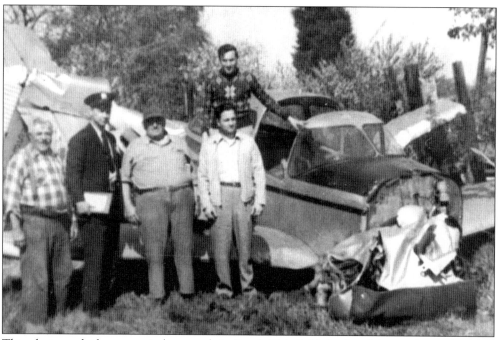

This photograph shows an airplane crash in South Plainfield. In the photograph are, from left to right, Mr. Risoli, Officer Eddie Tyler, George Downer, George Colantoni, and another unidentified individual at the crash of a North American Navion. These airplanes were manufactured from the late 1940s through 1951.

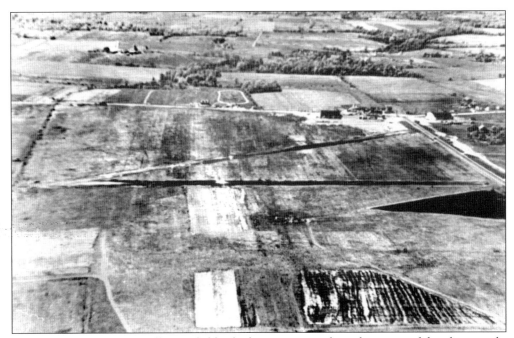

Here is a pilot's view of Hadley Airfield. The hangers are in the right center of the photograph. The two runways form a V and run across the center of the picture. Today, a modest granite memorial by the Holiday Inn on Stelton Road, near Route 287, marks where the airport once stood.

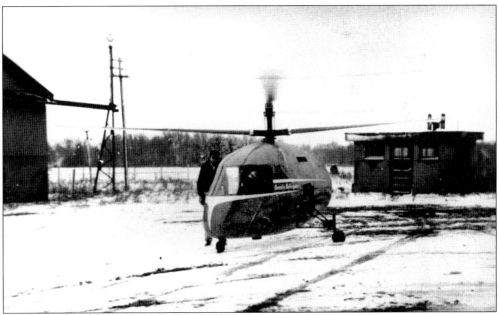

This is the Bendix Model K, an experimental helicopter that employed counter-rotating main rotor blades. Notice there is no tail rotor; the counter-rotating blades made it unnecessary. These helicopters were manufactured from 1945 until 1949 but never achieved certification. Bendix had hoped to develop a helicopter suitable for family use. Clearly, the idea never came to fruition.

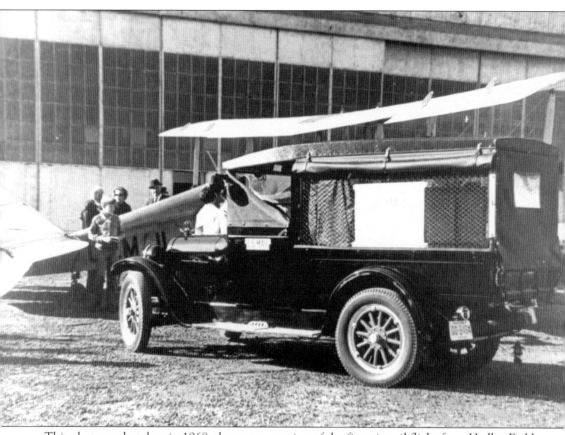
This photograph, taken in 1968, shows a recreation of the first airmail flight from Hadley Field. The airplane is a De Havilland DH-4. An early mail truck is in the foreground.

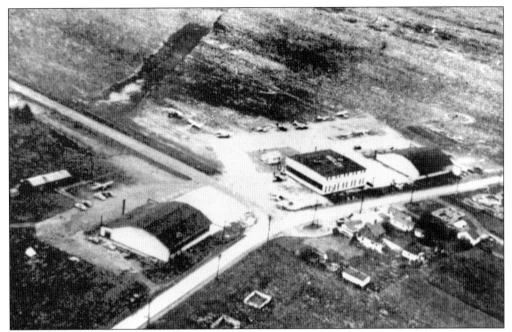

This photograph gives an aerial view of Hadley Field. The white line running across the bottom of the photograph is Stelton Road. Notice the two hangers flanking the shop in the center. A small miniature golf course is located at the right side of the photograph. Also note the string of foundations for houses being built along Stelton Road.

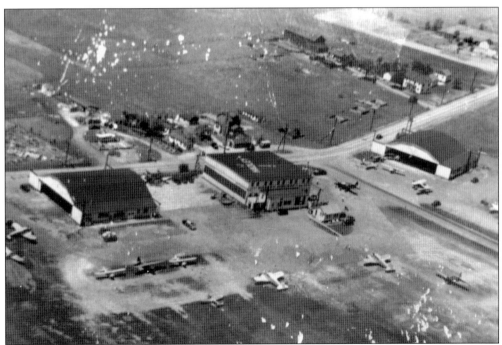

This is another aerial photograph of Hadley Field. This view shows the old Hadley farm in the upper right corner of the photograph. Today, this is a densely developed corner of South Plainfield.

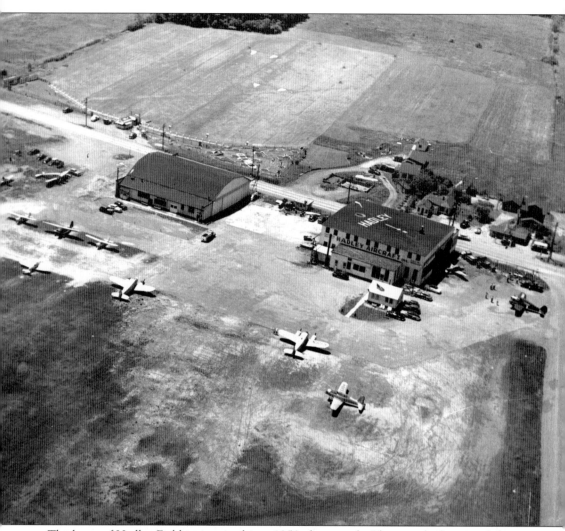

The heart of Hadley Field is seen in this *c.* 1950 photograph. The view looks toward the west. By this time, Hadley was functioning primarily as a general aviation field. Included in the photograph are several Cessna Bobcat twin-engine aircrafts. These had been used extensively as trainers and transports during World War II. The single-engine aircraft at the bottom right-hand corner of the photograph is a Consolidated Vultee Valiant. These planes were nicknamed "Vibrators" for their rough ride.

Six
IN SERVICE

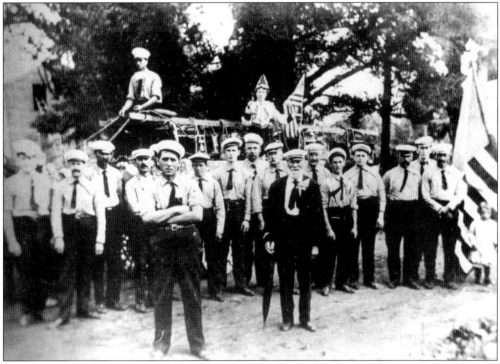

The South Plainfield Volunteer Fire Department was formed in 1907. This picture was taken shortly thereafter. William Hamilton Sr., the first fire chief and later the first mayor, is in the front with his arms folded. Seen to the right of Hamilton is Judge Bethune Dunham. The firemen in this photograph are, from left to right, Harold Tappan, Oscar Thorne, Ellis Shives, Robert Thorne Jr., Al Bruntage, Robert Thorne Sr., Walton Smith, Peter McDonough, Charles Brantingham, Martin Kaine, and Patrick Kaine. Monroe Pyatt is driving the wagon, a hose cart. The children are unidentified. Chief Hamilton, who was also a blacksmith, built the hose cart.

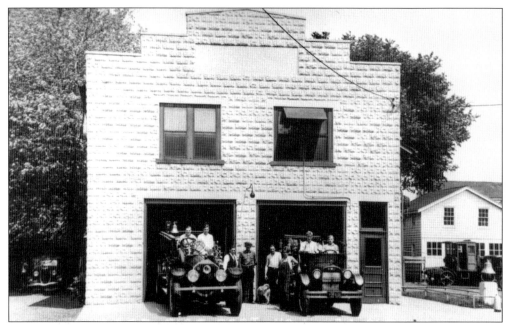

A group of young men informally pose at the fire department with two of the early engines. Notice the fire bell to the right of the station. The fire department purchased a chassis for a truck in 1917 and Chief Hamilton built a body for it. In 1926, an American LaFrance 600-gallon pumper was purchased. Up to this point, the firemen owned almost all of the firefighting equipment themselves.

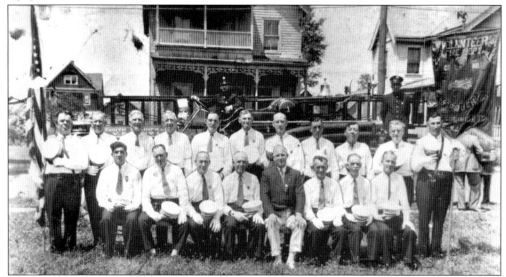

This is a photograph of the 10th anniversary of the South Plainfield Exempt Firemen's Association as photographed in 1931. Seen here are, from left to right, the following: (first row) Frank A. Diana, Nathan Snyder, Ed Sloan, Edward Ten Eyck Sr., Elvin Post, William Clancey, Louis Randolph, and Jeffrey Sofield; (second row) Frank Gubernaut, Floyd Austin, Oscar Thorn, William Wilson, Patrick F. Kaine, Harry Tappan, John Horne, Mr. Kisko, James Abbruzzese, Harry J. Manning, and Frank Phillips. Norman Sofield is at the wheel of the fire engine, and William Fritz is at the end.

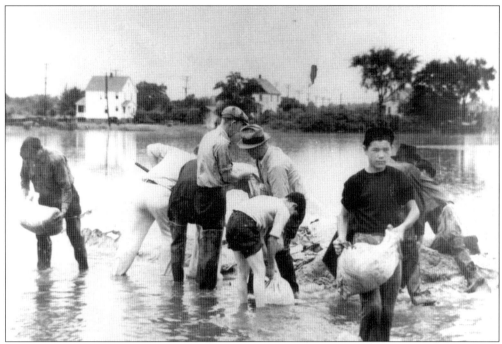

Here, a group of firemen are fighting the flood of 1936. The photograph was taken near Spring Lake on Plainfield Avenue. The sand bags do not seem to be doing the trick. Plainfield Avenue flooded regularly until the road was realigned in the 1970s.

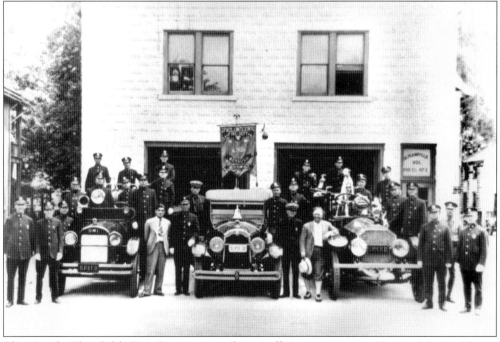

The South Plainfield Fire Department shows off its equipment. Notice Mayor Martin O'Loughlin (1933–1935) leaning on the fender of a fire engine and wearing spats. Today, the old firehouse is a dance school. It still stands on Hamilton Boulevard.

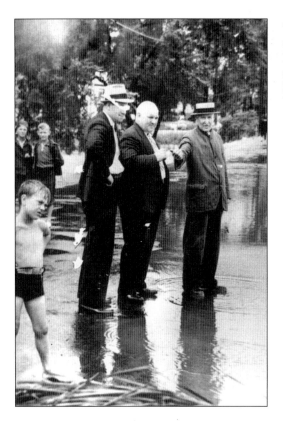

This photograph shows Mayor Ledden (on the far right) and two unidentified men on Plainfield Avenue surveying the damage during the flood of 1936. Ledden was South Plainfield's third mayor. Ledden Terrace is named after him.

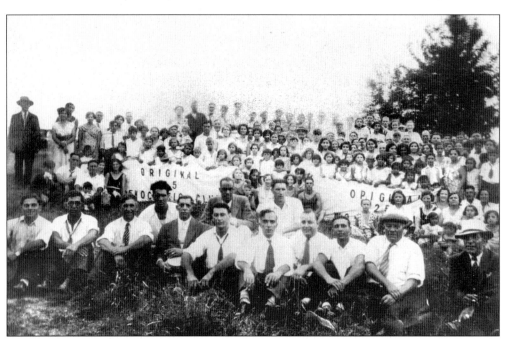

Here we see an outing of the South Plainfield Democratic Club at Lake Surprise in 1933. South Plainfield has had a strong Democratic organization for much of the 20th century.

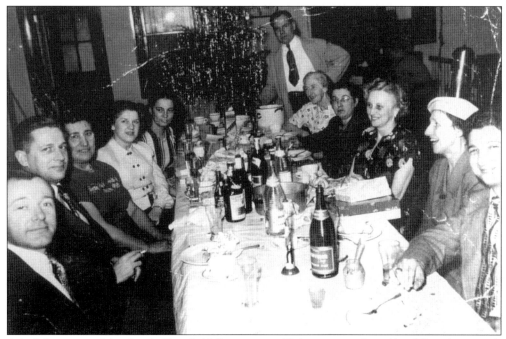

A holiday party of the South Plainfield Democratic Club is captured on film. This photograph dates from the 1930s.

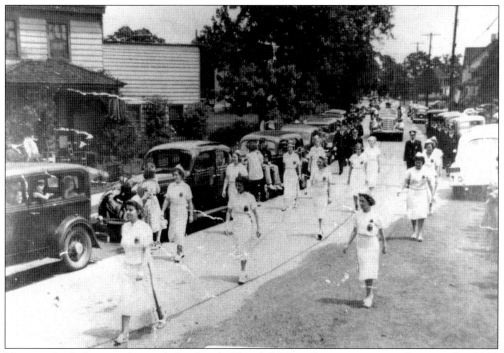

Here is the ladies auxiliary of the South Plainfield Fire Department marching in the 1939 Fourth of July parade.

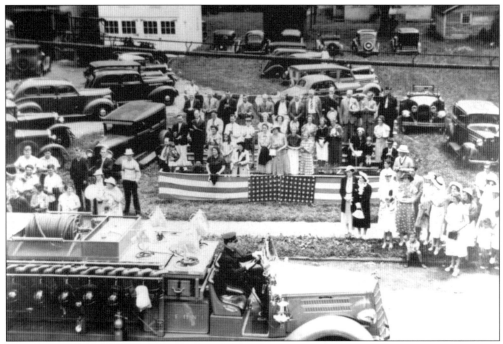

This is a photograph of the reviewing stand at the Fourth of July parade in 1939. Notice the new ladder truck driven by Tom Sloan.

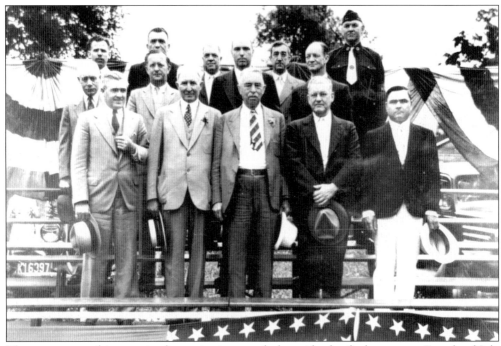

The town council is seen in the reviewing stand alongside the firehouse at a Fourth of July parade in 1939. Mayor Ledden is second from the left in the first row. Also pictured are Messrs. Phillips, Babes, Brantingham, Stilo, Sloan, Thornton, Manning, and others.

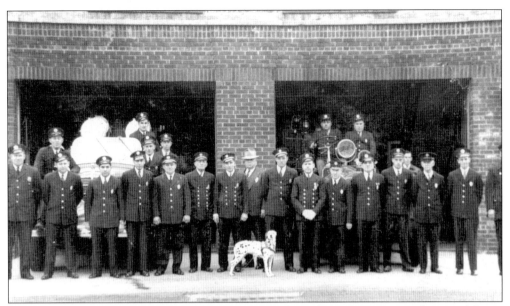

The fire department sent this postcard to all firemen from the town serving in the armed forces during World War II. This card was received aboard the CV USS *Randolph* in 1945. The *Randolph* was an aircraft carrier, which served in the Pacific Theater supporting the Iwo Jima invasion and the Okinawa campaign. The vessel was badly damaged by a kamikaze attack in May 1945.

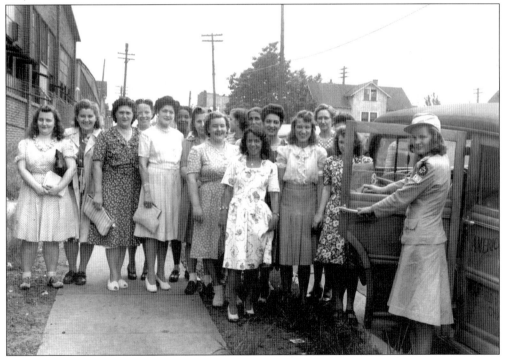

Here is a group of cheerful blood donors from Cornell Dubilier about to be transported to the Red Cross center in Plainfield. The photograph dates from 1946. (Courtesy of Mary Mazepa, South Plainfield Historical Society collection.)

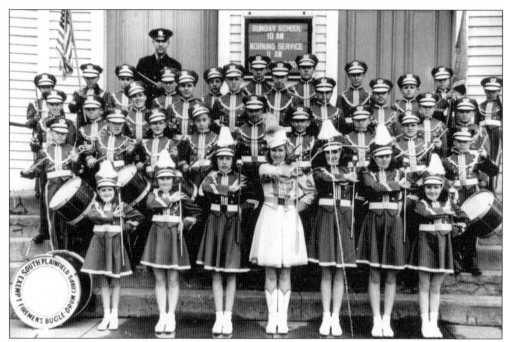

Seen here is the South Plainfield Exempt Firemen's Bugle and Drum Corp with the director, Chief Andrew A. Phillips, at the top left. Jackie Austin, the drum majorette is in the front in white. The photograph dates from 1942 and was taken on the steps of the Baptist church.

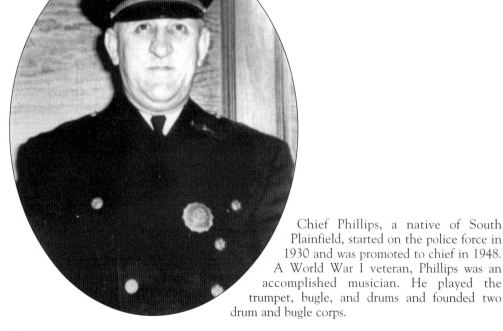

Chief Phillips, a native of South Plainfield, started on the police force in 1930 and was promoted to chief in 1948. A World War I veteran, Phillips was an accomplished musician. He played the trumpet, bugle, and drums and founded two drum and bugle corps.

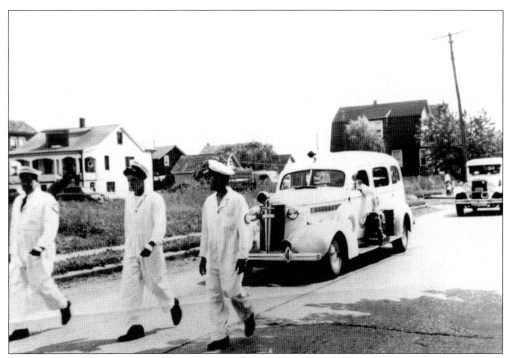
The South Plainfield Rescue Squad marches in a parade in the 1940s. The rescue squad was founded in 1943 and acquired its first ambulance in June 1944.

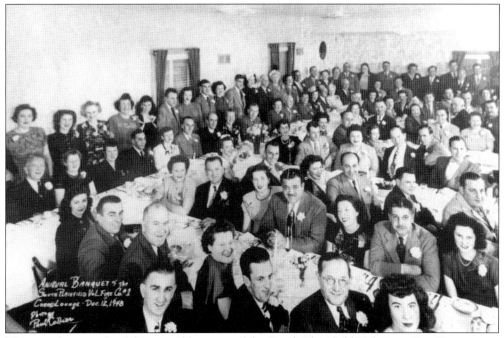
This is a photograph of the annual banquet of the South Plainfield Volunteer Fire Department in 1948. Everyone seems to have crowded in to the picture.

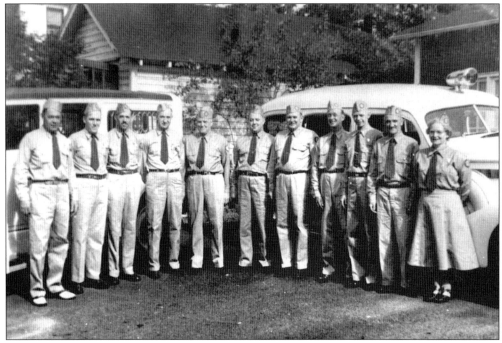
This 1940s photograph shows a group of Red Cross volunteers posed with two ambulances.

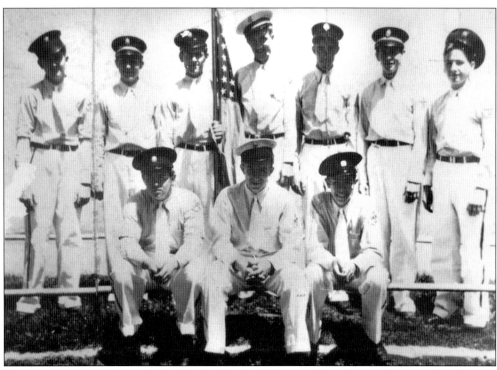
Here are some members of the South Plainfield Rescue Squad in a photograph taken in the 1940s.

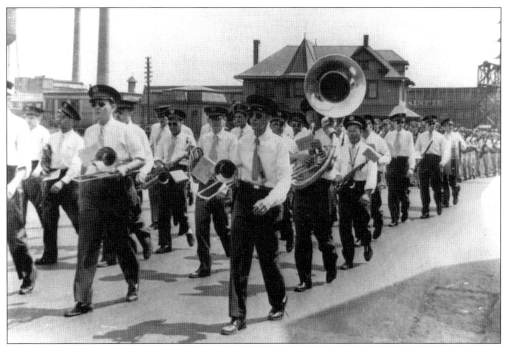

This parade photograph is from the 1940s. A drum and bugle corps, followed by a group of uniformed and armed soldiers, is passing by the train station.

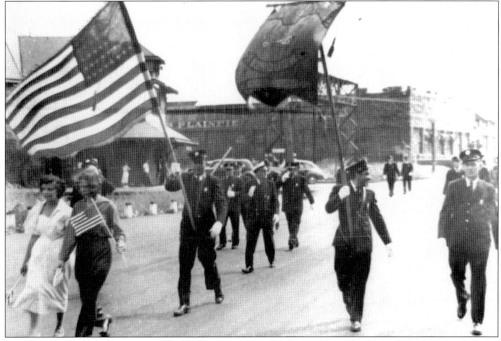

Another photograph, possibly from the same parade, shows a contingent of firefighters passing the railroad station. The Cornell Dubilier plant is in the background. The photograph was taken on Hamilton Boulevard.

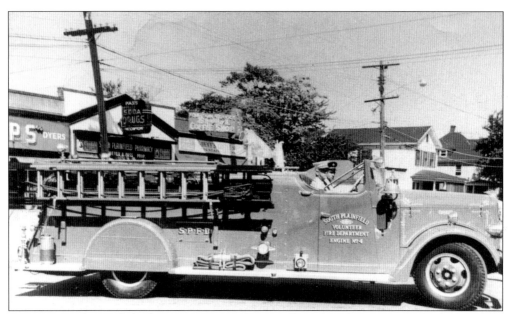

Two firemen show off the latest rig on Hamilton Boulevard in the 1950s. In the background, the South Plainfield Pharmacy and a coffee shop can be seen.

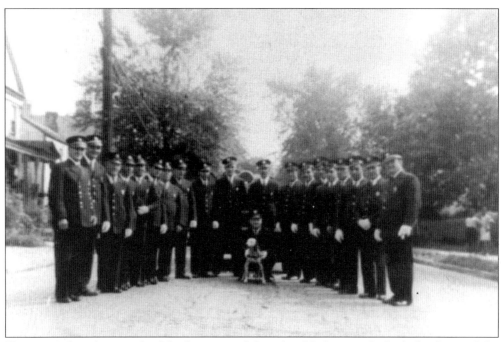

Here is another photograph of the firemen and their dog. Unfortunately, both the date and the occasion are unknown. As the men are wearing their white gloves and dress uniforms, it may have been a parade.

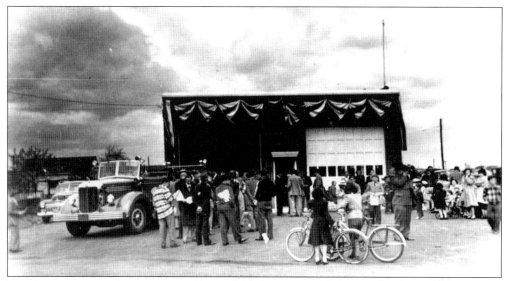

The sky seems to be threatening a deluge at the dedication of the new South Side Firehouse in 1949. The building stood on Hamilton Boulevard near Roosevelt Elementary School. It was torn down in the 1990s.

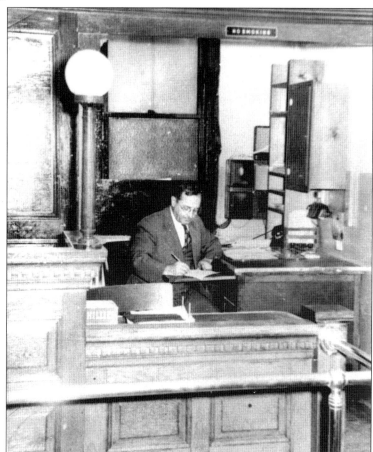

This photograph shows Charles Carone hard at work. Carone was one of the two original borough employees. He liked to refer to himself as the borough's "public information officer." He was the first borough clerk and also a member of the school board.

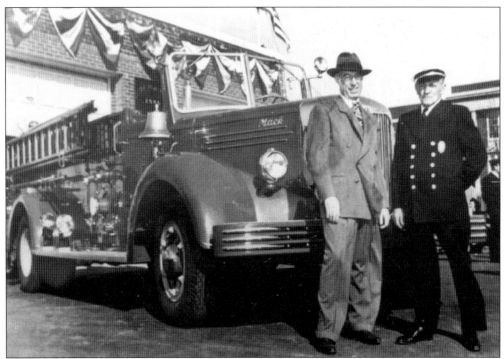

Chief Joe Delaney and Mayor Thomas Lee are seen at the dedication of the South Side Firehouse on April 24, 1949. Also pictured is a newly purchased 1,000-gallon-per-minute Mack pumper.

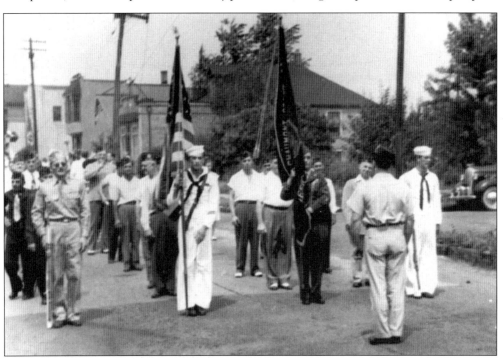

This is an undated parade photograph showing a group of veterans at a parade. South Plainfield has long been famous for its parades.

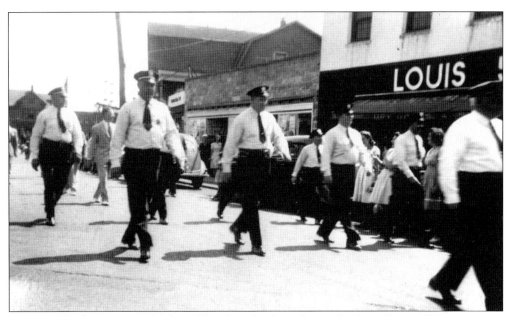

A group of policemen parade down Hamilton Boulevard past the Louis Five and Dime.

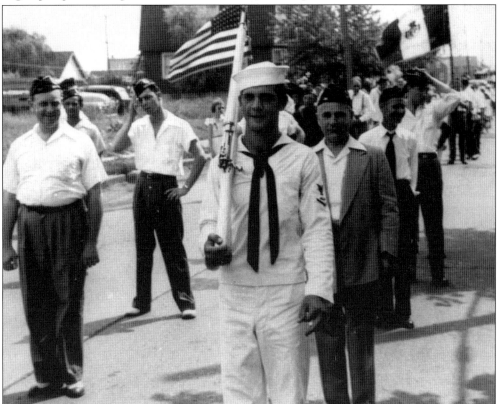

In this undated photograph, a contingent of veterans takes a break during a parade. The photograph probably dates from the 1950s. It would appear from the flags that the next group is from the Sons of Italy or the Italian-American Club.

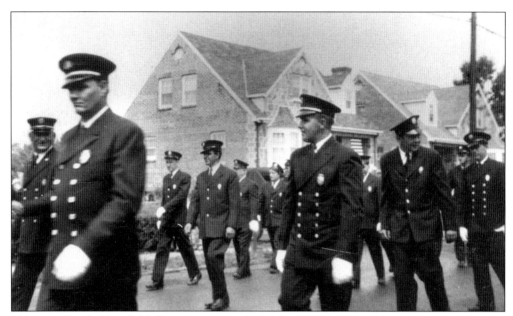
Here are South Plainfield firemen on parade in the 1950s. This photograph was taken on Hamilton Boulevard near Our Lady of Czestochowa Church.

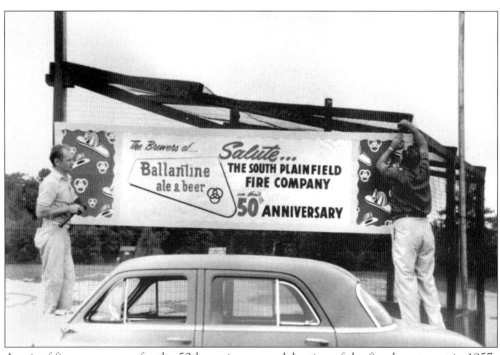
A pair of firemen prepare for the 50th-anniversary celebration of the fire department in 1957.

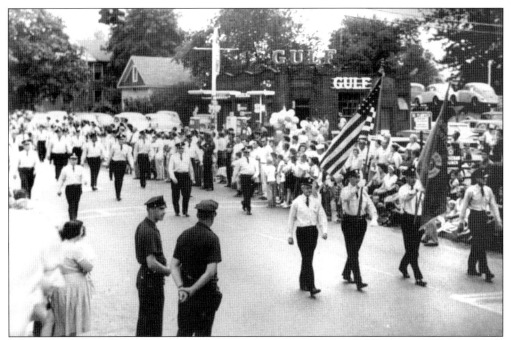

Here, firemen march in the 1960 Labor Day parade. South Plainfield's first Labor Day parade was held in 1957. Notice the load of brand-new Volkswagen Beetles behind the Gulf station.

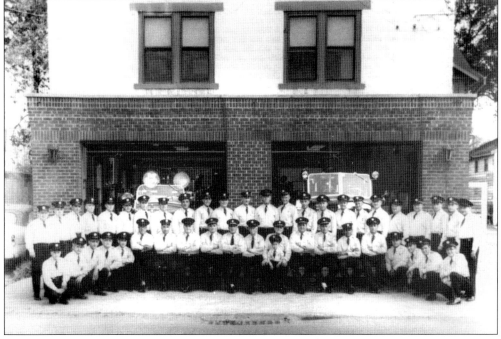

This is a view of inspection day at the fire department in 1956. Notice how much larger the fire department is at this time than it was during World War II. Presumably, this reflects the return of men serving in the armed forces and the town's growing population.

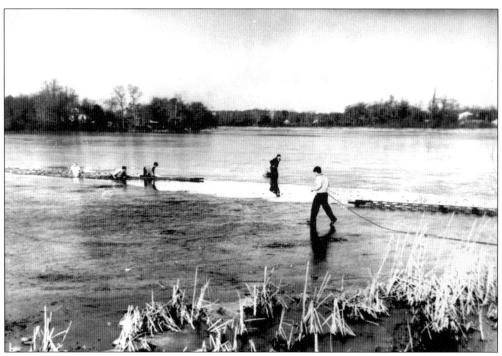

This 1960s photograph shows Chief Delaney and other members of the fire department rescuing two boys who had broken through the ice on Spring Lake.

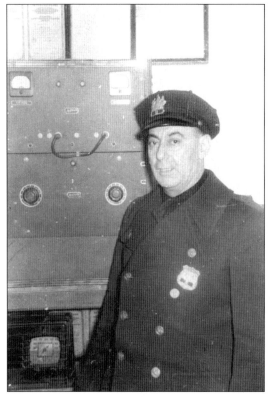

Here is Patrolman Scalera posing with the police department's new radio. This photograph, taken in the 1950s, shows the nerve center of the police department. The department has grown and changed considerably since those days.

Seven
School Days

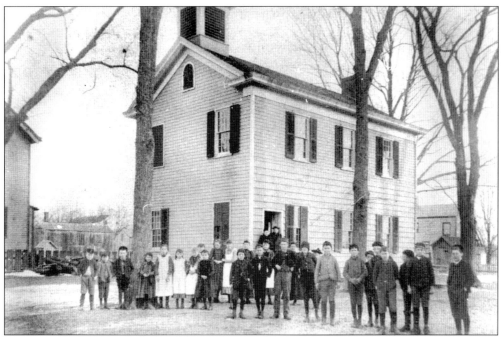

This is the old schoolhouse in the center of town. This simple frame building with a bell tower preceded Grant School, which was built in 1900. The photograph dates from the late 19th century. An outhouse can be seen to the right of the school, as can some of the houses and barns of New Brooklyn, one of the hamlets that grew to become South Plainfield.

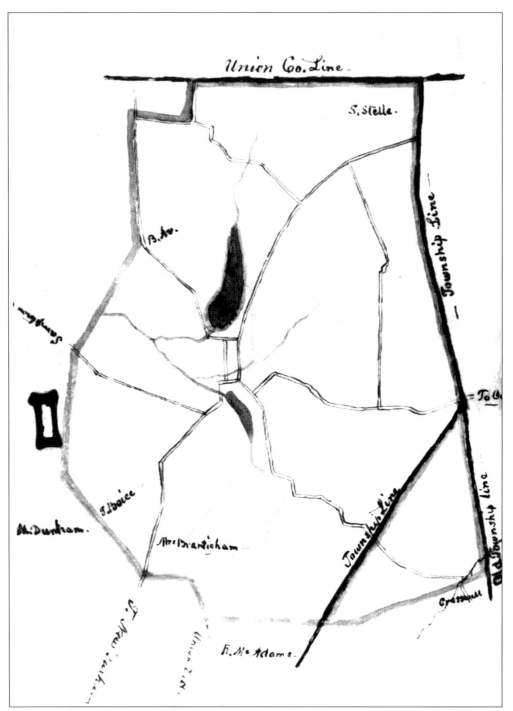

This is a hand-drawn map, dated March 12, 1872, showing the boundaries of school district No. 5, New Brooklyn. Ralph Willis, the county superintendent, was the cartographer. The map encompasses much of what today is South Plainfield. Note Spring Lake to the north and the sawmill pond to the south. The rectangle in the center of the map is the center of New Brooklyn.

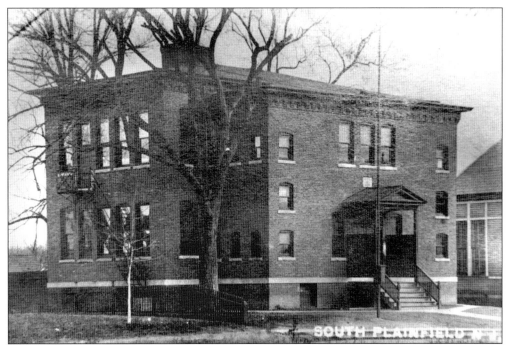

This 1914 photograph shows old Grant School viewed from Hamilton Boulevard. The Baptist church is located to the right of the school. The building was subsequently expanded and reoriented making the Front Street side the front.

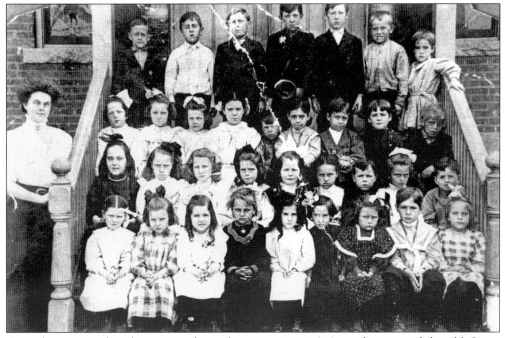

A somber group of students poses for a class portrait c. 1910 on the steps of the old Grant School. Notice the teacher to the left of the stairs, with a hair style and dress reminiscent of the Gibson girls.

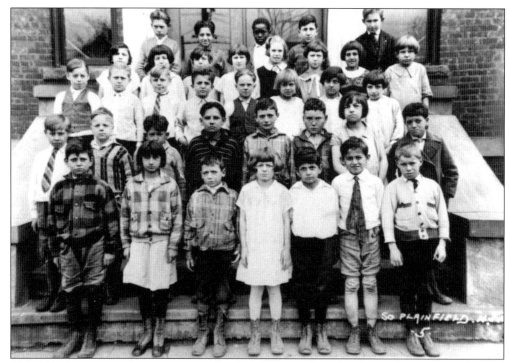

Here, another group of anonymous students poses for a photograph. Again, the Grant School stairs, now concrete and stone instead of wood, serve as the backdrop. The students appear no happier than their predecessors, though this photograph was taken in the 1920s. In 1929, there were 42 teachers in the South Plainfield school system. They included 9 college graduates, 27 were normal-school graduates, and 6 were "otherwise trained." Their average salary was $1,400 a year.

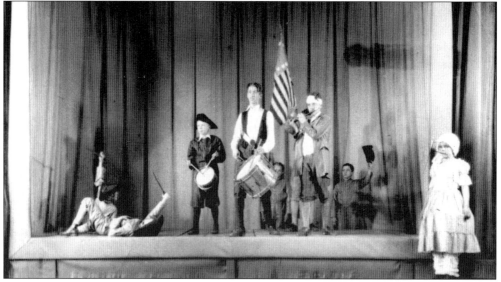

Students at Grant School perform the *Spirit of '76* in 1927. Apparently, this performance and the one depicted in the following photograph relate to the sesquicentennial celebrations. (Photograph by Howard Rowe.)

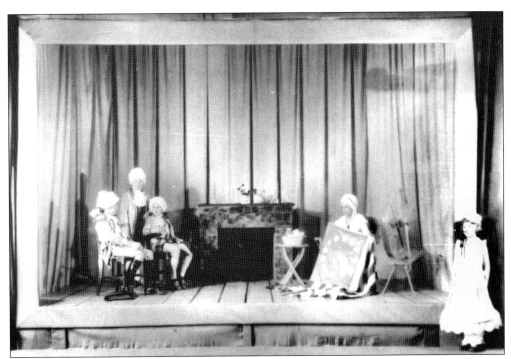

Here is another patriotic event at Grant School. The students are depicting Betsy Ross making the flag. This photograph also dates from 1927. (Photograph by Howard Rowe.)

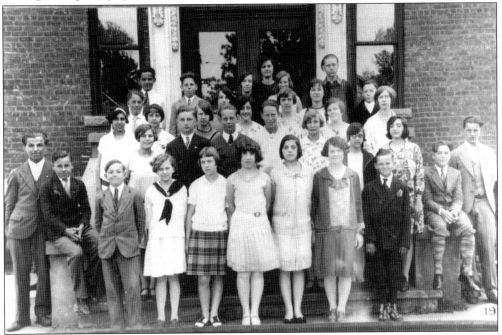

This is the Class of 1928 at the old Grant School. The young man standing at the far right of the picture is John E. Riley. Riley was hired as a teacher when he was only 19 years old, and he worked his way up to principal of the Grant School. Today, one of the borough's elementary schools is named after him.

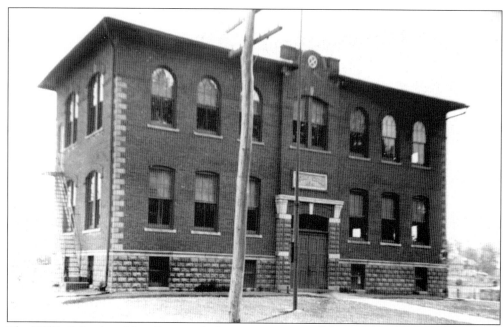

The Willis School on New Brunswick Avenue was originally a Piscataway Township school. Later, it served South Plainfield as an elementary school and as the school system's administration building. Today, it houses the New Life Christian School. It was built in 1891.

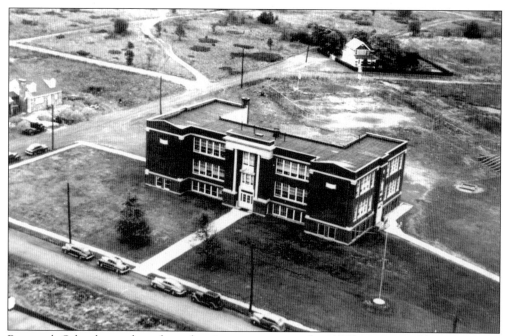

Roosevelt School, seen here from the air, was constructed in 1929 at a cost of $300,000. The lots on which it was built were purchased at a cost of $200 and $250 by the board of education. The school's initial enrollment was 425 students. This was the first school that South Plainfield constructed. South Plainfield had previously inherited three schools from Piscataway Township: Willis, Grant, and Columbus.

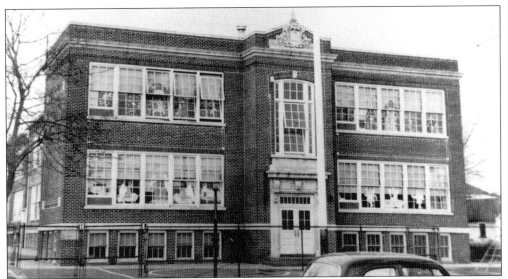

This photograph shows the new façade of the Grant School. It dates from the 1950s. The red brick building is decorated with buff-colored terra cotta. Note the playground in front of the school. Currently, this building serves as the Keystone Community Residence, a home for disabled youths.

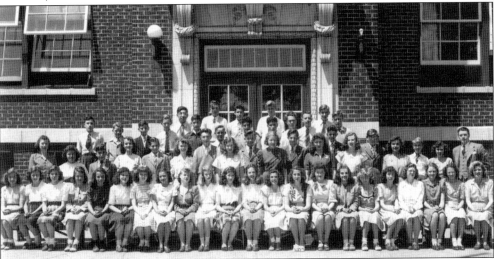

Seen here is the eighth-grade graduation at Grant School (the old Grant School) in 1947. The students are, from left to right, as follows: (first row) Victoria Lillo, Ann DeCarlo, Margie DePue, Starr Handville, Connie DeSouza, Alwayne Smith, Margaret Kling, Josephine Calangelo, Nancy Case, Carol Meeker, Dorothy Scarbaci, Nadia Zawadowsky, Nanette DeFillipo, Ina Smith, Grace Phelps, Gloria Morella, Mary Williams, Johanna Frace, Nancy Sorensen, Joan Menner, Frances Banul, and Mrs. Baker; (second row) Miss Flately, Janet Abbruzzese, Bob Valentino, Phyllis DeMarco, John Poole, Joan Mills, Donald McCann, Carolyn Rogg, Alex Pornivetz, Ruth Zimmerman, Bob Horned, Dolores Firovanti, Betty Case, Fred McClean, Dolores DeSouza, Ed McBridge, Cahterine Phillips, and Mr. Riley; (third row) Saverio Russo, James Morrison, Mark Richard, Ken Suydam, Russ Diana, John Juva, John DiAmica, Charles Hortabay, Bill Smith, Joe Kizimbo, and Fred Ungeretta; (fourth row) Alex DiAmico, Al Meissner, Frank Risso, John Gubernut, and Raymond Ketchum.

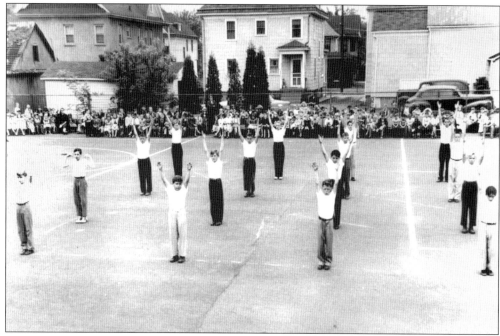

Here, students perform calisthenics on the playground at the old Grant School. Note the large number of spectators. The photograph dates from the 1950s.

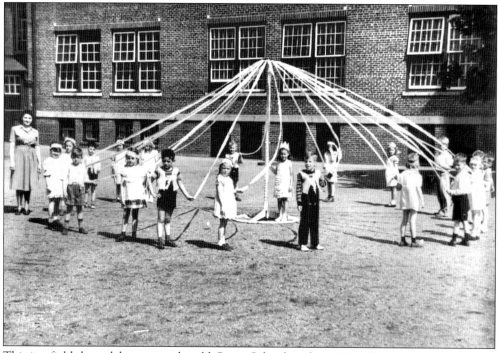

This is a field-day celebration at the old Grant School in the 1950s. The students are dancing around a Maypole.

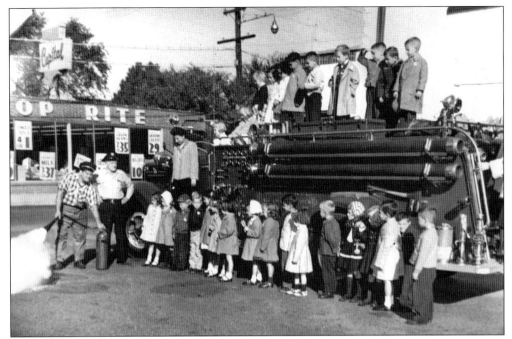

Students enjoy hands-on learning with Chief Delaney and an assistant as the firemen show off the department's equipment to a rapt audience in the 1950s.

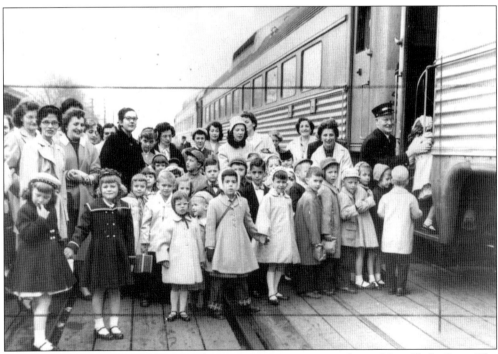

Kindergarten children, teachers, and parents enjoy a train ride to New York City. The photograph, which dates from the 1950s, was taken in Plainfield. They are about to board a train from the Central Railroad of New Jersey. The conductor seems to have his hands full.

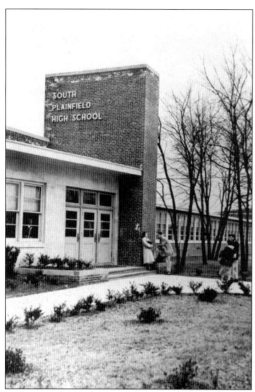

This 1957 photograph shows students chatting on the steps of South Plainfield's first high school. Before its construction, students from South Plainfield had attended North Plainfield High School. Today, the building serves as the borough's middle school.

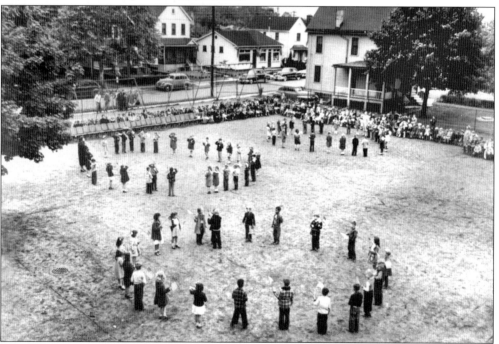

Another field-day event is seen at the old Grant School in the 1950s. Again, the games have drawn a crowd of spectators. The photograph also gives an idea of what downtown South Plainfield looked like in the 1950s.

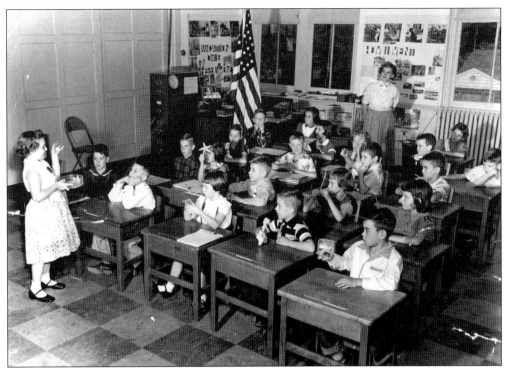

Here is a glimpse of show and tell at the Willis School in 1954. Pictured are, from left to right, the following: (first row) Dennis Ryan, Robert Brodak, Maryann ?, Bruce Ryno, and Bradley Powers; (second row) Eric Pear, Sandra Snedecker, Ronald Ketres, Barbara Gunderson, and Bethanne Keiner; (third row) Karen Hoffsmith, Fred Kirchhofer, and William Shultes; (fourth row) Janet Youcan, Ruth Ann, and John Bosco; (fifth row) Linda Halverson and Linda Bundshuch.

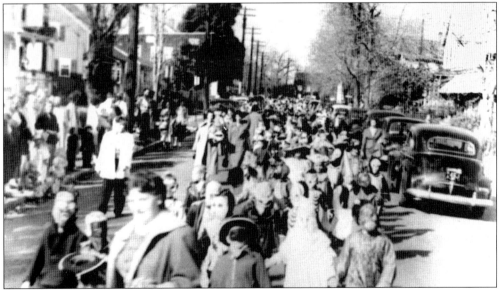

Halloween parades have been a staple of elementary school since the 1950s. This group of miniature ghouls and goblins is from the old Grant School.

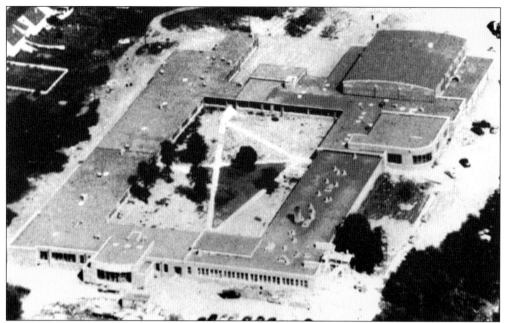

Here is the former South Plainfield High School on Plainfield Avenue as seen from the air c. 1957. Notice the cars parked in front of the building on what today is lawn. This photograph was taken shortly after the building was completed. Grass has not yet begun to grow back around it.

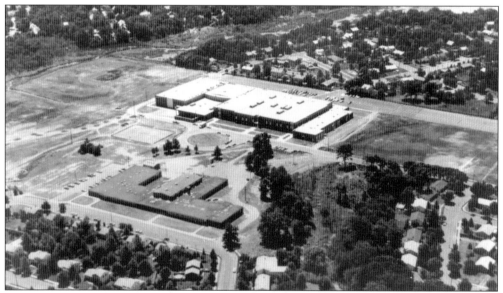

This is an aerial view showing the new Grant School in the foreground and the new high school in the background. Spring Lake is in the upper right corner of the photograph. When the new high school was constructed in 1973, it had open-space classrooms, carpeted floors, air conditioning, and was considered a model educational facility. The open-space classrooms proved to be better on the drawing board than in reality as they allowed noise to spill over from one class to another. The situation was rectified in the 1990s, when walls were built around the teaching areas.

Eight
SUBURBANIZATION

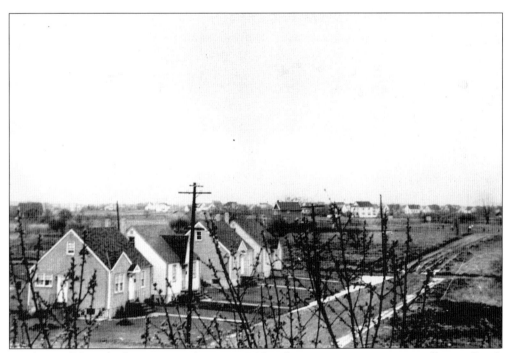

We have all heard of a "room with a view." New houses were springing up all over South Plainfield in the 1940s. This photograph shows the view from the third floor of 415 Garibaldi Place in 1949.

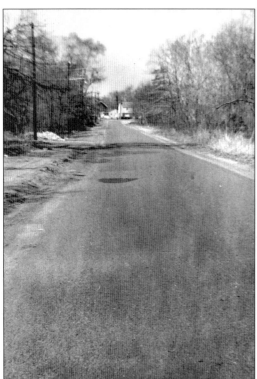

This photograph shows Franklin Avenue in 1957. The photograph, taken by Charles W. Beagle, borough engineer, was sent to the *American City Magazine* to illustrate Beagle's method of road construction. Franklin School would soon be built in the woods on the right side of the photograph.

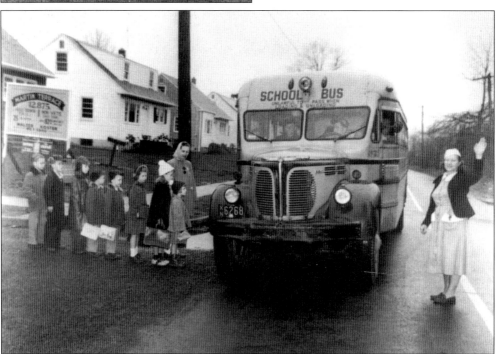

A crossing guard is holding traffic as students, lunch boxes in hand, board the bus. This photograph was taken in 1955. Note the price of the new homes on Martin Terrace, $12,875. Today, that number has multiplied by a factor of 20.

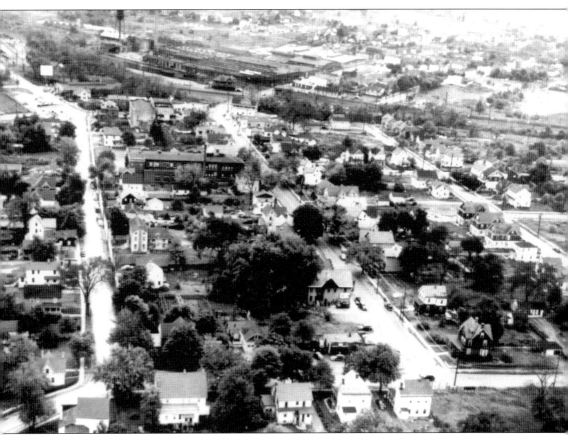

This aerial photograph from the 1950s shows downtown South Plainfield. The view looks toward the south. The road on the left side of the photograph is Front Street. Hamilton Boulevard parallels it to the right. The old Grant School, now the Keystone Community Residence, is near the center of the photograph. (Reproduced courtesy of the South Plainfield Public Library.)

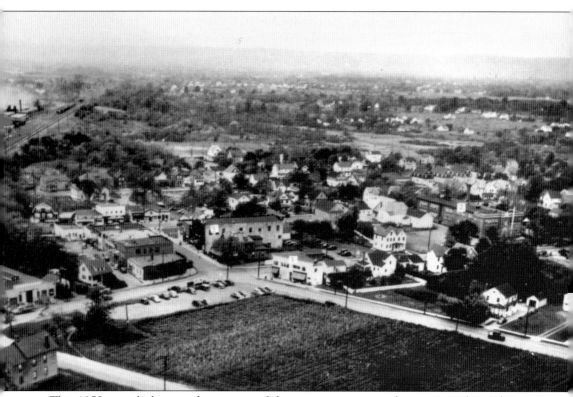

This 1950s aerial photograph was part of the same sequence as the previous shot. This view looks toward the northwest. The field in the foreground is now the Drug Fair parking lot. DeSabato's Theater is in the center of the photograph. Oak Tree Road is at the bottom of the photograph. (Reproduced courtesy of the South Plainfield Public Library.)

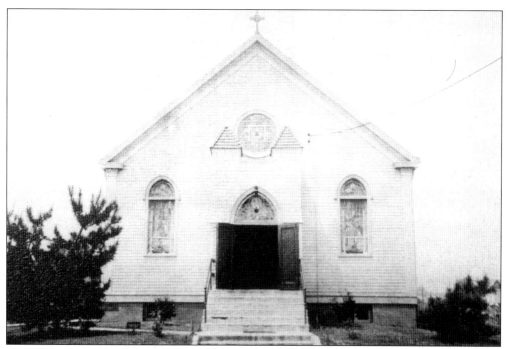

This photograph shows the first Sacred Heart Church. It was completed in 1907 and served the growing Catholic population in South Plainfield. Previously, Catholics had worshiped in Metuchen and Dunellen. In 1964, ground was broken for the present Sacred Heart Church, an imposing edifice of buff-colored brick and Indiana limestone.

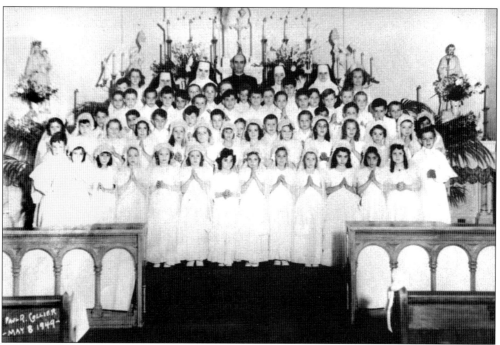

A confirmation class at Sacred Heart Church was photographed by Paul Collier in 1949.

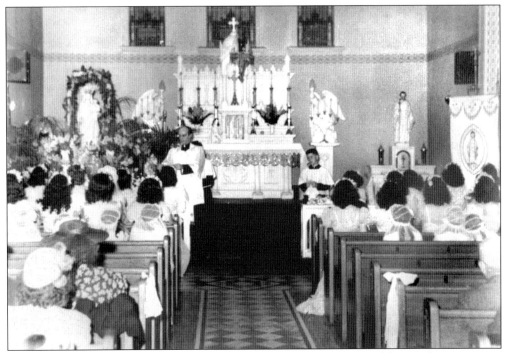

Here is another view of the interior of the old Sacred Hearth Church. Although the same priest is officiating, the interior of the structure appears to have been redecorated.

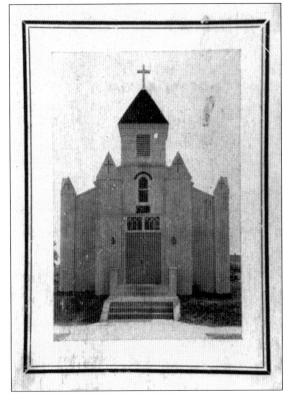

Our Lady of Czestochowa Church on Hamilton Boulevard was dedicated in May 1944. Its first pastor was the Reverend Ladislaus J. Madura. This photograph is from a souvenir card distributed at its dedication.

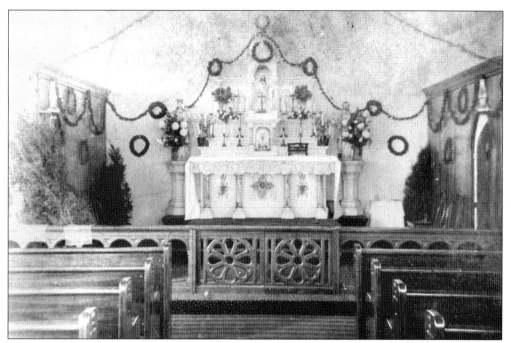

This is a view inside the old Our Lady of Czestochowa Church. This building was reputedly built, in part, with surplus lumber from Camp Kilmer. A new church replacing it was constructed in 1976.

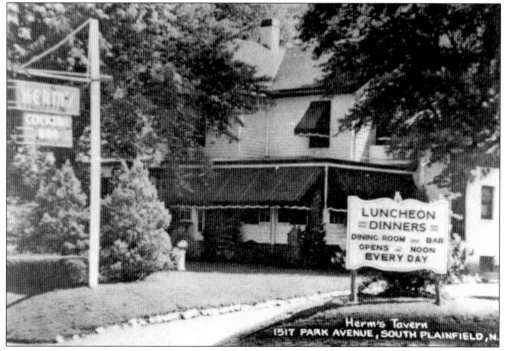

Herm's Tavern, at 1517 Park Avenue, was a popular eatery. Herman J. Frowery purchased it from a couple of bootleggers after the repeal of prohibition in 1935. He operated the restaurant for 41 years. A fire gutted it in 1977.

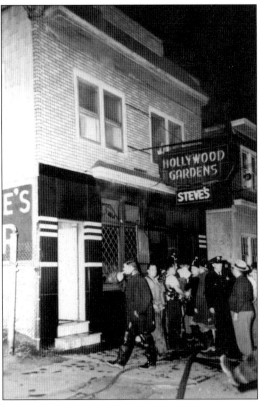

Hollywood Gardens, formerly known as Hollywood Hall and Steve's Bar, was located on Hamilton Boulevard near the Cornell Dubilier plant. Hollywood Hall opened on January 21, 1928, under the management of Frank DeFillipo. Entertainment was provided by the 30-piece band of the Plainfield Beavers. This 1950s shot shows the crowd after the fire department had extinguished a fire.

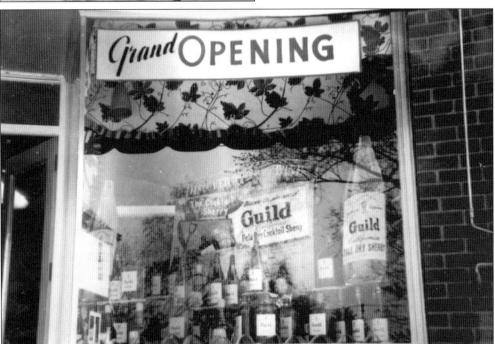

This view is of the South Plainfield Liquor Store on Hamilton Boulevard at its grand opening in 1952.

Mr. Katz, proud owner of the South Plainfield Liquor Store, poses at the opening. The current owner is William Thorn.

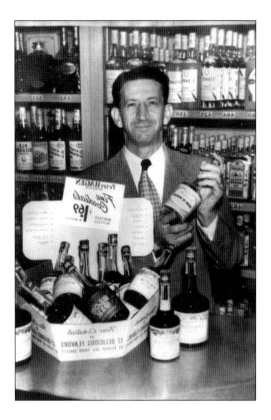

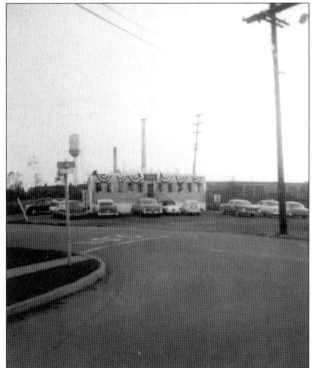

The parking lot is busy at Sherban's Diner in this 1950s photograph. Mr. and Mrs. Sherban opened the diner in the 1950s. In 1972, John Stellakis and Peter Ganiaris purchased the diner and considerably expanded it from the small chrome-clad structure seen here.

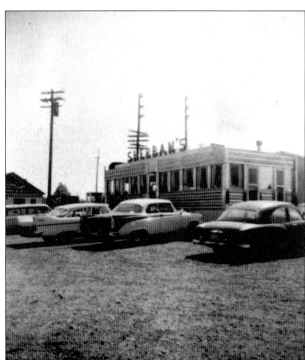

Cars with fins fill the Sherban's Diner lot in this early-1960s photograph. Note the Nischwitz store in the background.

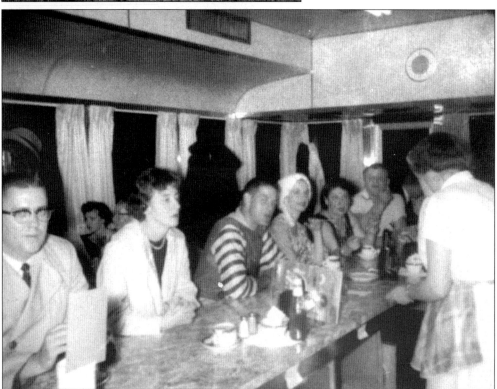

Every stool is filled in this 1960s photograph from Sherban's Diner. Mrs. Sherban is busy filling orders. Sherban's remains a popular eatery.

Bob Balfour, chief engineer of radio station WERA, AM 1590, starts up an auxiliary generator. For much of the 1960s, 1970s, and 1980s, South Plainfield had its own radio station. The antenna and studio of the station still stand on Oak Tree Road, but the site is slated for development in the near future.

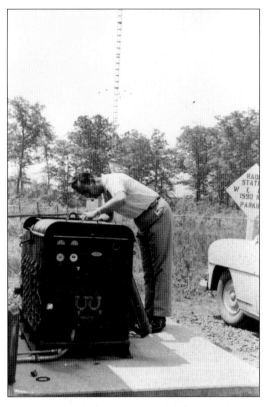

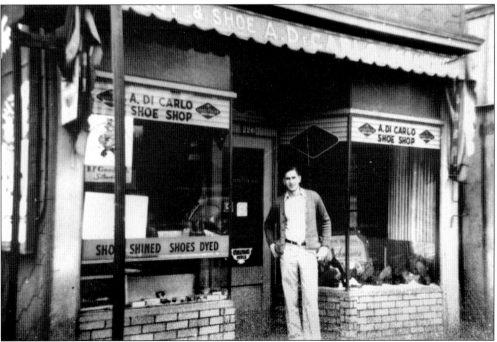

Seen here is the A. Di Carlo Shoe Shop on Hamilton Boulevard in downtown South Plainfield. This photograph was taken shortly after World War II.

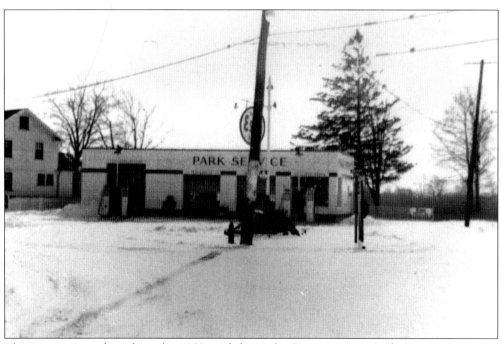

This wintry scene dates from the 1950s and shows the Esso station on Park Avenue.

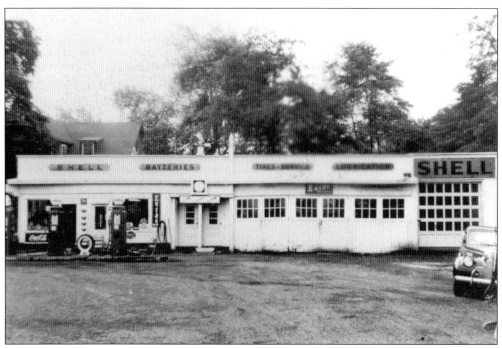

This Shell gas station was located on the corner of Plainfield and Maple Avenues. A new senior citizens center is now on the site.

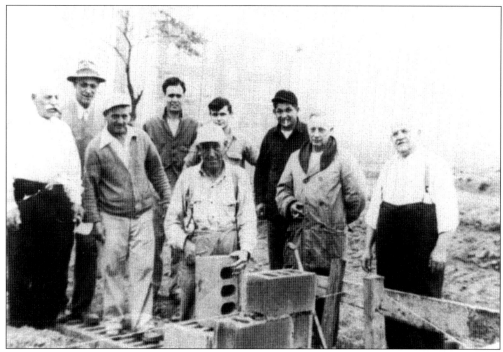

This photograph shows the laying of the foundation of the Italian-American Club on Jackson Avenue in 1954. Individuals in the photograph include Salvatore Testa, John Antelloni, John Celentano Sr., and others.

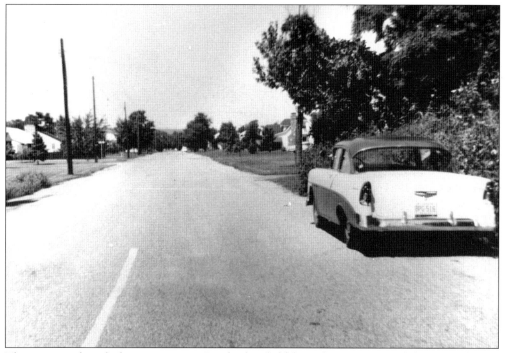

This is an unidentified street scene in South Plainfield from the 1960s. Ranch houses and roads have replaced the farms and fields.

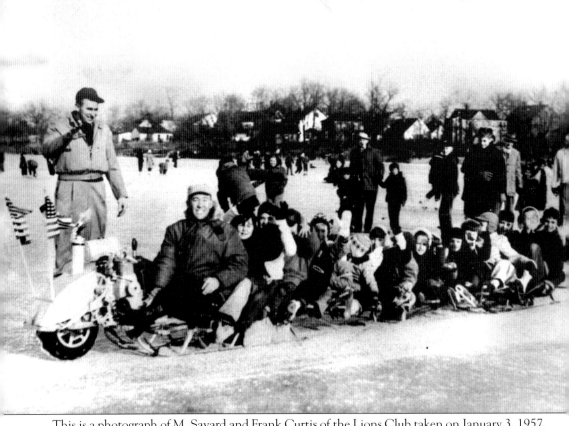

This is a photograph of M. Savard and Frank Curtis of the Lions Club taken on January 3, 1957. Frank Curtis constructed a power sled to tow sleds around Spring Lake. Apparently, he charged his passengers a small fee that supported the activities of the Lions Club.

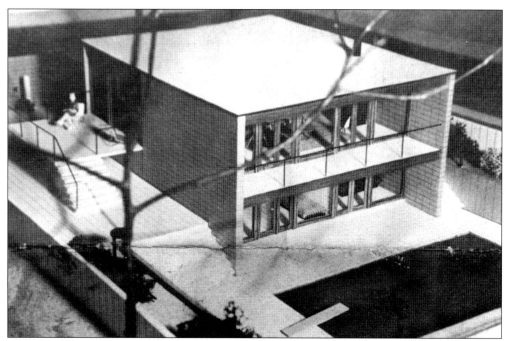

Although it is certainly not the oldest house in town, this unusual house on Risoli Terrace, built in 1961 by Nicholas Risoli and John Specht of R & S Builders, is an architecturally significant building. It won the grand prize in a contest to build an entirely concrete house. The house is over 90 percent concrete and includes freestanding concrete stairs and other innovative features. It was also the first total-electric home in New Jersey.

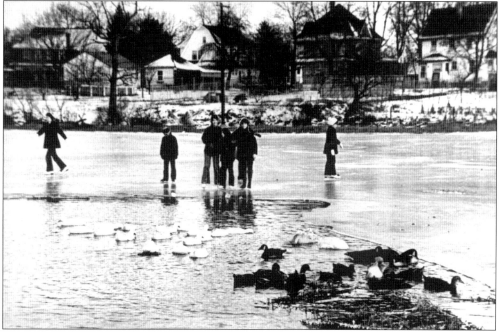

Youth knows no fear. These kids are skating on what appears to be very thin ice on Spring Lake. The ducks seem nonplussed.

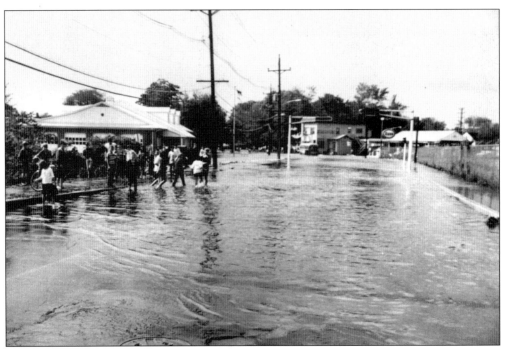

Plainfield Avenue is seen flooded again. This photograph was taken in the 1970s. The rescue squad is to the left.

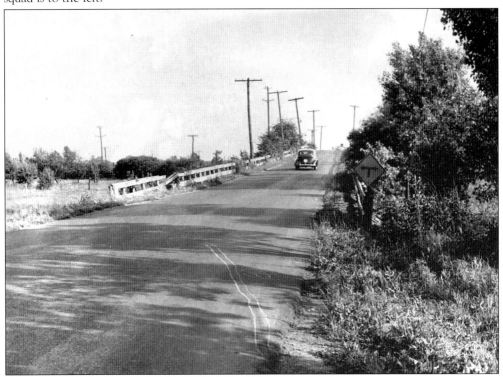

Seen here are the roads of home. This photograph shows the Hamilton Boulevard railroad overpass over the Port Reading Railroad in the 1950s.